NELSON'S SHIPS

a Trafalgar Tribute

Paintings and descriptive text by
Derek Gardner VRD RSMA

The life and work of Derek Gardner
by Ian Collins

www.messums.com

8 Cork Street, London W1S 3LJ
Tel: +44 (0)20 7437 5545

On Nelson's Canvas

I have served in the Royal Navy for some 38 years, a period of time in which I have had the honour to command four of Her Majesty's Warships and now a Fleet. Alongside such highs there have been commensurate lows but I have always felt the utmost pride to have fallen into the same career as that most exalted of British heroes – and the one to whose greatest victory Derek Gardner's latest exhibition is dedicated – Lord Horatio Nelson. Fortunately for me, my career was not forged in the harsh school that was the Eighteenth Century Fleet; the rigours of Nelson's world are not mine and no officer or sailor alive today can truly know the hardships with which their spiritual ancestors had to contend. Sails and cannon have become turbines and missiles, signals and despatches are now instant global communications and the beauty of sail has been hardened to grey painted steel.

Such differences notwithstanding, I rather feel that Nelson would be very much at home with modern maritime warfare. While the anti-submarine operations of the Cold War would have been indubitably alien to him and set-piece battles between great ships will not be repeated in my lifetime, the Royal Navy is now – once again – an expeditionary force with truly global reach. Littoral warfare and the ability to insert forces quickly and from afar are firmly embedded as a central tenet of RN doctrine. Consequently, there is a synergy between the troopships of Nelson's fleet and our newest Amphibious platforms, HMS ALBION and BULWARK. Trade by sea (approximately 90% of all movement of marketable product globally), and the maintenance of such trade in the face of piracy have again become priorities. Our ships, stationed as they are throughout the world have – in the last five years alone – assisted in the face of both nature's adversity and man's hostile action in locations as far removed as the West Indies, Sierra Leone and Sri Lanka. Remarkable similarities.

Our Navy is then drawn very much upon a canvas set by Nelson and to him, both as a Navy and a country, we owe a huge legacy that must not be allowed to diminish. This exhibition in 2005, 200 years after Trafalgar, is part of sustaining the corporate memory and is a fitting reminder of Nelson's life, victories and sacrifices. However, without the benefits of a camera, it is only through the skill of Derek's brush and his assiduous attention to historical detail that our 'memories' of this era continue to grow.

I first met Derek many, many years ago and David Messum has captured well a remarkable man who came to his career as a professional marine artist only late in life after success first as a civil engineer, gallant Royal Navy officer and – again – civil engineer. For me, his paintings capture a Navy, time and world long gone but one with which we still have much in common. Quite correctly, and as much as to the ships he paints so well, Derek draws our attention to the sea upon which they sail; an unpredictable partner with which any island nation must cast its lot. Therefore, in this 'Year of the Sea' and for the next 200 years, we ignore it only at our considerable peril.

Admiral Sir Jonathon Band KCB
Commander-in-Chief, Fleet

Derek Gardner

Index of Paintings

ISBN 1 903438-80-2 Publication No: CLXXXIX
Published by David Messum Fine Art
© David Messum Fine Art 2005 © Derek Gardner   Text © 2005 Studio Publications

The Studio, Lords Wood, Marlow, Buckinghamshire. Tel: Marlow 01628 486565
Photography by Robert Cotton
Printed by Clarendon Printers Ltd., Chesham, Bucks.

To my wife Mary
with my love and devoted thanks for her help
and encouragement over many years.

NELSON'S SHIPS a Trafalgar Tribute

Paintings and descriptive text by Derek Gardner VRD RSMA

The life and work of Derek Gardner VRD RSMA by Ian Collins

Salt-water has been said to run in the veins of Britons, whose islands and deepest identity are shaped by the surrounding sea. Ebbing and flowing around us, the liquid source of our protection and our prosperity is also the route of ancestral migration. None of us now lives beyond striking distance of the coast to which, from earliest childhood, we long to return. In the most popular British fantasy hazy summer holidays merge into sunny retirement with a sea view. And looking out from cove and cliff, sandy beach, marsh and mudflat, we love to scan the vast infinity of a watery horizon – on which may yet be traced the silhouettes of ships. Some claim that this defining perspective has produced in our European nation a mindset adrift somewhere in the mid-Atlantic, but in truth it anchors us in a sturdy independence. Even in a risk-averse era, our enviable setting – from sea to shining sea – continues to spring on us an age-old spirit of adventure.

Born in the land-locked county of Buckinghamshire, on February 13 1914, Derek George Montague Gardner first opened his eyes on a world in which Britannia ruled the waves – if only for a few more months of peace. Secured through the 1805 Battle of Trafalgar, at which Admiral Nelson had succumbed to his wounds only when assured of his victory, British mastery of the seas had ensured naval supremacy and mercantile might. These in turn had produced a Victorian empire extending over a quarter of the globe and an industrial muscle flexing across the continents. Although an arms race was well underway between the great powers of Europe at the start of 1914, none could have imagined that by August the murder of an Austrian Archduke, after his

1. **His Britannic Majesty's 64-gun ship "Raisonnable"** (detail opposite)
   Watercolour 10 x 15 ins, 25 x 38 cms Signed

   Nelson served in "Raisonnable", March to May 1771

The 64-gun ship "RAISONNABLE"

The RAISONNABLE, named after a French prize taken in 1758, was launched at Chatham in 1768. She was Nelson's first ship to which he was appointed as a twelve year old midshipman in March 1771. His uncle, Maurice Suckling, the ship's captain, was soon afterwards appointed to command the 74-gun ship-of-the-line THESEUS and on transferring to her in May he took his young nephew with him.

The RAISONNABLE saw much varied service in the course of a long career of forty-two years. She was with the Channel Fleet and on the North American station during the American War of Independence. After lying up in ordinary for ten years after the war, she was again put into commission when war with France broke out in 1793. Once more she was one of the ships of the Channel Fleet before taking part in the expedition of 1801 to the Baltic which led to the Battle of Copenhagen.

Her active years of service came to an end in 1810 when she was paid off and became a receiving ship. She was finally broken up in 1815.

In this painting the ship is shown with the frigate VIRGINIA astern when in 1779 she was the flagship of Commodore Sir George Collier, Commander-in-Chief on the North American station.

His Britannic Majesty's 64-gun ship "Raisonnable". Launched at Chatham 1768. This was Nelson's first ship.

carriage took a wrong turning on a visit to Sarajevo, would pitch the world into a war whose bitter legacy ravaged the 20th century.

Derek's father was an eminent civil engineer who, at the end of the First World War, received a posting to Grimsby. His appointment as Docks Engineer for the Great Central Railway gave the family a new billet in Lincolnshire and his son an introduction to the nearby maritime scene which would become an abiding passion. "I often went with my father to look at the ships and was taken under the care of the various foremen," he recalls. "Even as an eight-year-old I was transfixed." Although determining to become a civil engineer, like his father, he learned the thrill of intense observation and started to hone the skill of recording, with pencil and paper, all the hustle and bustle of the great spectacle of shipping and the sea. Tellingly, the youngster fell for the romance of sailing ships even as technology was steaming ahead and he was looking forward to playing a professional part in it. These early forays into the art of draughtsmanship would stand him in good stead at Oundle School in Northamptonshire, where he was soon sent as a boarder.

He has written: "I have always enjoyed drawing and am indeed thankful in being blessed with such a gift. Nowadays a good deal of emphasis in our schools seems to be placed on Art, but when I was a schoolboy it was very much an also-ran subject and was referred to simply as Drawing – which is just about as far as it went. Even so I seem to have been handy enough with a pencil as I still have a handsome red leather-bound book with our school crest embossed on the cover which I won at the age of 14 for Drawing. The book, Notes on the Science of Picture Making, by Sir Charles Holmes, one-time Director of the National Gallery, was an inspired choice on somebody's part because in the years ahead it became a source of much interest and understanding when, in my twenties, I began to experiment with paint."

In 1928, when Derek was 14, his father became Chief Engineer of the Port of Glasgow and the Clyde Navigation Trust.

2. **His Britannic Majesty's 74-gun ship "Triumph"** *(detail opposite)*
Watercolour 5½ x 8½ ins, 13 x 20 cms   Signed

Nelson served in "Triumph", May to July 1771

10

The 74-gun ship "TRIUMPH"

The TRIUMPH was launched at Chatham in 1764 during a period of peace. It was not commissioned until May 1771 by Captain Maurice Suckling – Nelson's uncle who, on transfer from the RAISONNABLE, took his thirteen-year-old nephew with him. As the vessel was moored as guardship on the Medway there was no prospect for the young Nelson gaining sea experience so his uncle sent him in a merchant ship on a voyage to the West Indies and back. Nelson returned to the TRIUMPH just over a year later and remained in her until July 1773 when he went to the bomb vessel CARCASS on an expedition to the Arctic.

In December that year she was paid off and for almost the next five years she was again laid up until required for service and recommissioned in November 1778. Fifteen months of convoy escort work in the Channel was followed by transfer to the West Indies where she served until returning to England for a major refit in July 1782. With the war coming to an end in November 1782 the TRIUMPH, after a year as guardship at Portsmouth, spent long periods either laid up or under repair before being commissioned for war service in November 1794. In June 1795 she was one of the ships with Vice-Admiral Cornwallis which, encountering a far more powerful and numerous French fleet off the Britanny coast, were saved from defeat by his skilful handling. The action became known as Cornwallis's Retreat and became a Battle Honour.

The TRIUMPH continued operating in the Channel until the end of 1796 when she was sent to Admiral Adam Duncan's North Sea fleet keeping watch over the Dutch fleet in the Texel. They put to sea in October and were brought to action in one of the fiercest encounters of the wars at the Battle of Camperdown which resulted in the capture of eleven out of the eighteen ships in Vice-Admiral de Winter's line. Like all the ships involved in that hard-fought battle, the TRIUMPH was heavily damaged with over eighty casualties.

After repairs at Portsmouth she served with the Channel Fleet but after the short-lived peace of 1802-03 she was sent to join Nelson in the Mediterranean. She returned in August 1804 to Portsmouth to refit. After recommissioning and service in the Channel in July 1805 she was one of the ships in Vice-Admiral Calder's force which intercepted Villeneuve's fleet returning from the West Indies. Two Spanish ships were captured but fog was largely the cause of the action being only a limited success. The TRIUMPH had a number of casualties and considerable damage to her hull and rigging. After repairs she went to the Channel Fleet again, Captain Sir Thomas Hardy – Nelson's Hardy – being her commander for three years from May 1806.

The ship was showing signs of her age by 1810. She was paid off, cut down and became a hulk at Milford being finally broken-up at Pembroke in 1850.

His Britannic Majesty's 74-gun ship "Triumph". Launched 1764.
Battle Honours: Cornwallis Retreat 1795, Camperdown 1797, Calder's Action 1805, Basque Roads 1810.

Amid all the grime and the smoke this was a glittering advance on the rail depot and fishing fleet of Grimsby. For vessels of all kinds had been built on the Clyde for centuries, until the pioneering spirit of the steam age turned the waterway into the world's greatest ship-building centre. Dozens of celebrated ship yards contributed to the development of steam power, with many innovations in construction and design. More than 20,000 ships have been launched there over the last two centuries (each one now detailed on the website www.clydebuiltships. co.uk). Between 1900 and 1938, in the era of triple expansion engine steamships and turbine ships, the rollcall covered launches, barges, dredgers, sloops, coasters, colliers and cargo vessels, trawlers and tankers, tugs and pilot tenders, steam yachts and paddle steamers, ferries and liners, lightships and hospital ships, battleships, frigates, cruisers, destroyers and minesweepers. Each vessel went on to chart a unique story of service and adventure until all but a small flotilla were scrapped or sunk. The latter casualties included the Royal yacht Alexandra – renamed Prince Olaf and blitzed during the Nazi invasion of Norway in 1940 – and the Cunard liner Lusitania, torpedoed by the Germans off the west coast of Ireland, in 1915, with the loss of 1198 lives.

Between the wars the busy River Clyde teemed with activity, even in the prolonged period of economic depression – firing the imagination of the young Derek Gardner. As thousands of men toiled in the dockyards, wharves and warehouses, the sounds of banging and hammering and the showering sparks of furnaces and welding tools produced all the drama of firework displays in an ants' nest. Such scenes would be depicted in the World War Two Port Glasgow paintings of Stanley Spencer. Although the Clyde continues today as a hub of ship-building, with three surviving yards working to naval and specialist commissions, the Gardners were present at the end of an era when toiling masses, engaged on the construction of vast vessels, recalled the raising of a pyramid. The ghost of such

3. **His Britannic Majesty's 24-gun frigate "Seahorse"** *(detail opposite)*
Watercolour 10 x 14 ins, 25 x 36 cms Signed

Nelson served in "Seahorse", October 1773 to March 1776

14

The 24-gun frigate "SEAHORSE"

This frigate was one of the first of the improved cruisers to carry their main battery on one deck, the two or three lower deck gunports of earlier Sixth Rates being omitted in this new design.

The ship was launched at Harwich in 1748 with a main armament of twenty-two nine-pounder guns on her upperdeck and two four-pounders on the quarterdeck. The first ten years of her service seem to have been uneventful, no doubt with duties escorting convoys and keeping watch over our merchant shipping but in 1759 she was one of a large expedition taking the army over to the St. Lawrence to attack the French at their stronghold at Quebec. In September General Wolfe's brilliant tactics led to the defeat of Montcalm's army and Canada became a British possession.

The SEAHORSE returned to England in December and after refitting at Deptford and working with the Channel Fleet she sailed for the East Indies in February 1761 where she took part in the operations which resulted in the capture of the port of Manila in the Philippines. On her return to England the ship was paid off and laid up for the next eight years. She came back into service in 1771 and went to the West Indies where she remained for eighteen months before returning to Portsmouth to refit and prepare for further service in the East Indies. It was as she was lying at Spithead prior to her departure that Midshipman Nelson joined her in October 1773. He served in her under captain George Farmer until 1776 when, at Bombay, he was taken seriously ill with fever. It was

considered imperative to send him home. It so happened that the 24-gun frigate DOLPHIN was about to sail for England to refit and arrangements were accordingly made for the invalid to take passage in her.

The SEAHORSE went on to see much service in the East Indies sailing with the fleet under Vice-Admiral Sir Edward Hughes and taking part, no doubt, as signal repeating frigate in five battles against the French under Suffren for which the ship was accorded the following Battle Honours: Trincomalee 1782, Sadras 1782, Providien 1782, Negapatam 1782 and Cuddalore 1783.

The war ended, she came home to Deptford in 1784. Being thirty-six years old and no longer required, this hard-worked little frigate was sold.

His Britannic Majesty's 24-gun frigate "Seahorse". Launched 1748.
Midshipman Horatio Nelson served in this ship, October 1773 to March 1776.

awesome assemblies may be found today at Chittagong, in the Bay of Bengal, where ships, like beached whales, are broken down into scrap by swarms of labourers who have yet to hear of the words health and safety.

On leaving school, in 1931, he began his training as a civil engineer in Glasgow – first with the London Midland & Scottish Railway and later in the drawing office of Sir William Arrol & Co, the firm which built the Forth Bridge. For a short time he worked for the celebrated shipbuilders Barclay Curle & Co, helping to construct engines for the ship Port Chalmers which later took part in one of the war-time convoys sent to relieve Malta.

In 1934, at the age of 20, he joined the Royal Naval Volunteer Reserve as a midshipman, and started to paint watercolour pictures of the warships on which he might be expected to serve. Around this time he read Robert Southey's Life of Nelson which began what was to become a life-long interest not only in Nelson but in the broad scope of naval history. Over the past five decades many of Derek Gardner's paintings and watercolours have been of the ships and battles of the Nelson era and in the exhibition of his work covered by this catalogue there are watercolour drawings of many of the ships in which Nelson served.

*　　*　　*　　*

Born in the Norfolk village of Burnham Thorpe, in 1758, Horatio Nelson had enlisted in the Royal Navy at the tender age of 12, becoming a captain's coxswain at 15, a lieutenant on a frigate four years later, and at 21 taking command of HMS Hinchinbroke in the West Indies. A hail of stones thrown up by an enemy cannon ball robbed him of his right eye in 1794, but failed to halt his progress. Made a commodore in 1796, Nelson was promoted to rear admiral and knighted the following year. His right arm was sacrificed during the attack on the Spanish at Santa Cruz de Tenerife in 1797 – the year before he was made a Baron for his

4. **His Britannic Majesty's 24-gun frigate "Dolphin"** *(detail opposite)*
Oil 10 x 16 ins, 25 x 41 cms Signed

Nelson served in "Dolphin", March to November 1776

The 24-gun frigate "DOLPHIN"

This ship had an unusually varied career during her twenty-five years in the Royal Navy. Launched at Woolwich in 1751 and after active service in the Seven Years War (1756-63), she was one of the first ships taken in hand and sheathed experimentally with copper as protection against the damage caused to wooden hulls by the toredo worm. In 1769 she was sent out as an expedition ship to the Pacific and so completed a voyage of circumnavigation. In the seventies she was sent out to the East Indies but by 1776 it seems she was much in need of a refit and was ordered to return to England. It so happened that Midshipman Horatio Nelson then serving in the frigate SEAHORSE was seriously ill with fever and his captain considered it imperative for him to return home. He was accordingly taken into the DOLPHIN and under Captain James Pigot's care was brought back to England where he made a good recovery.

My painting shows the DOLPHIN coming up Channel in September 1776 off Berry Head at the time when Nelson was an invalid on board her.

Evidentally no longer suitable for service she went to the breakers in 1777.

His Britannic Majesty's 24-gun frigate "Dolphin". Launched 1751.

outstanding victory at the Battle of the Nile. After the collapse of the Treaty of Amiens in 1803, Nelson was appointed commander-in-chief of the Mediterranean fleet and set on course for Trafalgar.

A courageous and inspirational commander, Nelson led from the front – as his catalogue of injuries (and his stoical response to constant sea-sickness) bore witness. In 1804 he blockaded the French Mediterranean ports, knowing that Napoleon's plan to invade England depended on the formation of a Franco-Spanish fleet large enough to defeat the Royal Navy. A year later the enemy ships broke free, sailing for the West Indies in a vain attempt to concentrate their forces for an invasion. Nelson pursued his foes across the Atlantic and back before engaging them off the Spanish coast – near Cape Trafalgar.

Although the combined French and Spanish forces outnumbered Nelson's fleet by 33 ships to 27, he cut the odds by launching a surprise attack in two columns at right angles to the enemy line. In the thick of combat, Nelson, remaining fully visible as usual in order to inspire his men, was spotted by a French marksman. The sniper's bullet struck him in the shoulder, passed through his lung and shattered his spine. Mortally wounded, he was taken below deck, lingering on for three hours in agony until he received the news that the Franco-Spanish fleet was routed. "Kiss me, Hardy," he said to Victory's captain (or, just possibly, "Kismet, Hardy"). And then came his famous last words: "Now I am satisfied – thank God I have done my duty."

National jubilation on news of the Trafalgar triumph was matched by an outpouring of grief over the loss of Lord Nelson at the age of 47. His body was borne home in a cask of brandy, lying in Greenwich's Painted Hall before a state funeral, on January 9 1806, at which the Prince of Wales led the mourners. Huge crowds joined the procession or lined the streets of London as the hero's coffin inched towards St Paul's Cathedral. There,

5. **His Britannic Majesty's 64-gun ship "Worcester"** *(detail opposite)*
Watercolour 10 x 15 ins, 25 x 38 cms Signed

Nelson served in "Worcester", October 1776 to April 1777

The 64-gun frigate "WORCESTER"

The WORCESTER is seen here escorting a convoy of merchantmen when on passage to Gibraltar in January 1777. Horatio Nelson was serving in her at that time having joined the ship as her 4th lieutenant at Portsmouth the previous October. She remained on convoy work throughout a winter of very bad weather. On returning to Portsmouth in April Nelson left the ship and hastened to London for his examination as Lieutenant which he successfully passed and next day received his commission as Second Lieutenant of the frigate LOWESTOFFE.

The WORCESTER was launched at Portsmouth in 1769. She saw much action in the course of twenty years, serving under Admiral Keppel at the Battle of Ushant in 1778 and later gaining Battle Honours for Sadras, Providien, Negapatam in 1782 and at Cuddalore in 1783.

She came home in 1786. Being no longer required for normal service the ship was paid off and a year or so later was hulked, finally being broken up in 1816.

His Britannic Majesty's 64-gun ship "Worcester". Launched 1769.
Horatio Nelson served in this ship as 4th Lieutenant from October 1776 to April 1777.

after the funeral service, it was carried to the crypt and placed in a 16th century Italian sarcophagus of black marble originally earmarked for Cardinal Wolsey. Some 47 years later that last resting chamber would be shared by the body of the Duke of Wellington, who had defeated Napoleon, finally and forever, at the 1815 Battle of Waterloo.

*   *   *   *

In 1938 Derek was appointed Assistant Docks Engineer at North Shields on the River Tyne. This 19-mile tidal river, extending from Hedwin Streams to Tynemouth harbour, had been a major route for the shipping of coal from the 13th century – and the produce of Durham and Northumberland mines would continue to be exported until late into the 20th century. Moreover, ship-building was as important to Tyneside following the industrial revolution as it was to Glasgow. The river was extensively re-modelled during the second half of the 19th century, so that Newcastle,

Wallsend, Gateshead and Jarrow could boom through the sweated business of docks and shipyards. Derek was based at the Albert Edward Dock, itself one of the great feats of Victorian engineering. When he arrived the tide of traffic was still dominated by colliers labouring to and from the port of London, but the yards had turned from the production of all manner of commercial vessels to the frantic building of warships. In August 1939, weeks before the outbreak of war, the engineer was called up for naval service.

He was sent north, to Scapa Flow in the Orkneys – the great natural harbour which was the main anchorage of the Royal Navy in both world wars, and the place where the interned German fleet was scuttled in 1919. He says: "Working on small trawlers, I was one of the officers in the Scapa Examination Service, whose duty it was to check all shipping other than warships entering the Flow." Given the harsh weather conditions usually prevailing in the Pentland Firth, this was a great experience for seamanship. "We

6. **His Britannic Majesty's 32-gun frigate "Lowestoffe"** (detail opposite)
Watercolour 10 x 14 ins, 25 x 36 cms Signed

Nelson served in "Lowestoffe", April 1777 to July 1778

The 32-gun frigate "LOWESTOFFE"

The design of the LOWESTOFFE was adapted from a French frigate, L'ABENAKISE, captured in 1757. She was launched at Deptford in 1761 with a main armament of 26 12-pounder guns and in the course of her forty-year service in the Royal Navy she had the reputation of being exceptionally fast, fourteen knots being recorded on one occasion which was unusual in those days. She saw much service in the West Indies during the American War of Independence and it was during this time that Nelson was her second lieutenant from April 1777 until July 1778.

The most outstanding action of her career took place in the Mediterranean in June 1795 when, in company with the small 28-gun frigate DIDO of only 9-pounder guns, the two ships engaged two powerful French frigates, L'ARTEMISE, 36 and LA MINERVE, 40, and after a gallantly fought encounter of over three hours duration, captured LA MINERVE the other ship escaping due to the severe damage to the two British frigates.

In August 1801, when escorting a convoy in the West Indies, the LOWESTOFFE went aground during the night off Great Inagua Island and became a total loss which at a subsequent Court Martial was blamed on a change in the direction of the current. All on board, totalling 215, were taken off safely.

His Britannic Majesty's 32-gun frigate "Lowestoffe". Launched 1761.
Lieutenant Horatio Nelson served in this ship from April 1777 to August 1778.

used to bob alongside a towering merchant ship, then clamber up the side on a rope ladder to talk to the captain on the bridge," he recalls. "After that I was never seasick again."

In the spring of 1942 Derek's war began in earnest, when he went to Portsmouth to join HMS Broke as an anti-submarine officer. That was a key posting for the Shakespeare class destroyer attached to the Western Approaches command, escorting Atlantic convoys on a hazardous passage harried by U-boats. In October the Broke switched to an Arctic convoy, accompanying the battle fleet to help in the relief of Russia.

Having weathered the war in the Atlantic and Arctic, the Broke was then sent to the Mediterranean to assist the landings in North Africa which were designed to trap Rommel's armies in a pincer movement. Along with the destroyer Malcolm, the Broke was given the task of securing the port facilities and power station at Algiers, and to prevent acts of sabotage from occupying Vichy French forces. "We charged the boom

at 25 knots just as daylight was coming, expecting it to be mined," Derek remembers. "But there was no explosion. We broke the boom and landed our troops, but the French brought up mortars and guns and we came under heavy fire. I went ashore to deal with a fire in a warehouse close alongside from which much smoke from burning sugar was causing us problems."

He continues the story: "Vichy resistance strengthened with the bringing up of mobile guns and mortars. As the ship was being hit as she lay alongside the quay, the only course left open was to retire. This we then did under heavy gunfire, sustaining many hits as we cleared the harbour. We were told to return to Gibraltar under escort, but the gallant Broke sank the next day when under tow by the destroyer Zetland – which, by expert handling, rescued those on board without any loss of life." Returned to a now-pacified Algiers, the crew finally headed for England on board a Dutch liner as part of a vulnerable convoy. En route they duly

7. **His Britannic Majesty's 50-gun ship "Bristol"** *(detail opposite)*
Watercolour 8 x 12½ ins, 20 x 30 cms Signed

Nelson served in "Bristol", July to December 1778

The 50-gun frigate "BRISTOL"

The BRISTOL was launched at Sheerness in October 1775 as one of eleven ships of the Portland class. On commissioning later that year she sailed for the West Indies where she served for the next six years during the War of American Independence.

Nelson was an officer in the BRISTOL for five months from July to December 1778. At that time she was the flagship of the Commander-in-Chief, West Indies, Rear Admiral Sir Peter Parker, who appointed him in September to be the ship's first-lieutenant. Three months later he was promoted to Commander and took over the 14-gun brig-sloop BADGER.

The BRISTOL finally came home to refit in September 1781 and the following year sailed for India where she served until 1786. This was the end of her sea-going career. Fifty-gun ships were by then considered not powerful enough to serve with the fleet and the BRISTOL became a hulk until broken up in 1810.

His Britannic Majesty's 50-gun ship "Bristol". Launched 1775.
Seen as the flagship of Rear-Admiral Sir Peter Parker in September 1778 when Horatio Nelson was the 1st Lieutenant.

suffered a U-boat attack – the aircraft carrier directly ahead of the liner being torpedoed and going down without a single survivor.

Derek Gardner was mentioned in despatches for distinguished service during the storming of Algiers – with further honours for the captain of the Broke, and the ship's doctor whose injuries included the loss of an arm. Derek came away with another souvenir: a loss of hearing in one ear due to the ferocity of the gunfire. But in 1943 he was back on the Western Approaches, on board the destroyer Highlander, for the decisive battle of the Atlantic – after which Admiral Doenitz finally withdrew the remnants of his U-boat fleet in the wake of crippling losses. As his hearing impairment worsened, Derek was then forced to leave the sea and join the staff of the Commander-in-Chief of Western Approaches, Admiral Sir Max Horton, in Liverpool. He was promoted to Lieutenant Commander.

The end of the war in Europe was followed by a posting to Ceylon. And with a further promotion to Acting Commander, Derek served as Assistant Chief Staff Officer to Rear-Admiral James Mansfield, Flag Officer, Ceylon, in Colombo, until the end of 1946 – some 15 months after the dropping of the atomic bombs and the Japanese surrender. On his retirement from the Navy, the Admiralty granted him the rank of Commander for his war service. With his innate modesty and complete lack of pomp, he adds: "I seldom use the title. I'm very happy with Mr."

Early in the war he had begun to make sketches of naval vessels in watercolour. At first he had little idea what he was doing, but deftness gradually came through diligent practice. His fascination with the challenge of depicting ships only deepened amid all the restrictions of war. He says: "You were allowed to do it as long as you sent the resulting pictures to the Admiralty for approval, where there would be checks that you hadn't included radar aerials and other sensitive equipment. The studies were returned, if acceptable, with an official stamp

8. **His Britannic Majesty's 12-gun brig sloop "Badger"** *(detail opposite)*
Watercolour 9¼ x 12 ins, 23 x 30 cms Signed

Nelson served in "Badger", December 1778 to June 1779

The 12-gun brig sloop "BADGER"

Horatio Nelson was twenty when appointed to command the BADGER at the naval base at Port Royal, Jamaica in December 1778. This was his first commissioned command which he held until June the following year when early promotion to Post Captain led to his transfer to the frigate HINCHINBROKE.

The BADGER'S history before she was brought into the Royal Navy in 1776 is not known but she was in all probability an American prize. Armed with twelve 4-pounder guns and swivels she spent the whole of her seven years of naval service in West Indian waters. During the six months when Nelson commanded her, the BADGER spent much of her time at sea on the lookout for American privateers. When Nelson left the BADGER she was taken over by Commander Cuthbert Collingwood. Years later, in October 1805, as a Vice-Admiral he was Nelson's second-in-command of the British fleet with his flag in the ROYAL SOVEREIGN at the Battle of Trafalgar.

In my painting I have shown the BADGER under reefed topsails.

His Britannic Majesty's 12-gun brig sloop "Badger".
Commanded by Lieutenant Nelson December 1778 to June 1779.

on the back. I used to give mine away to anyone who admired them. Now I'm told that they turn up at auction from time to time."

But an amateur artist still needed a professional career so he returned to the familiar field of civil engineering, albeit in an entirely new setting. He joined the Colonial Civil Service and travelled out to Kenya in 1947, revelling in a fresh opportunity in a continent known only from the mayhem of Algiers. Of this period he has written: "I have sometimes been asked if my engineering background has been useful in my later and much longer career as a professional artist. I think perhaps it has been because in painting I work whenever possible from old ships' plans and have developed a way of interpreting them to give a true perspective result. It was during my years in Kenya that in my spare time I really got down to the business of teaching myself to paint. Working in oil, watercolour and sometimes pastel, I exhibited both landscape and marine paintings in the lively shows of the Kenya Arts Society in Nairobi. In 1958, while still in East Africa, I had the good fortune and encouragement of having for the first time two of my paintings accepted for the annual exhibition in London of the Society of Marine Artists."

Kenya proved the perfect posting for another reason. In 1950, as chairman of the Naval Officers Association of East Africa, Derek had helped to organise the customary dance as part of the up-country entertainment for officers from H.M. ships arriving at Mombasa. This particular party was attended by a nursing sister, on leave from King's College Hospital in London, who had recently arrived with a wish to see something of the world. It was on that occasion that Mary and Derek met for the first time. They were married the following year. Kenya, it was decided, would be their marital home.

The couple moved from Nairobi up country to the shores of Lake Victoria, at Kisumu, where Derek was to be based as Regional Engineer for all of western Kenya.

9. **His Britannic Majesty's 28-gun frigate "Hinchinbroke"** *(detail opposite)*
Watercolour 10 x 14 ins, 24 x 36 cms Signed

Nelson served in "Hinchinbroke", June 1779 to May 1780

The 28-gun frigate "HINCHINBROKE"

This ship was captured in 1778 as the French L'ASTRÉE and taken into the Royal Navy as the 28-gun frigate HINCHINBROKE. Horatio Nelson, who had been promoted to Post Captain in June 1779 while commanding the brig BADGER, was appointed captain of the HINCHINBROKE taking over at Port Royal, Jamaica, in September 1779. Four months later he received orders to escort a military expedition to attack the Spanish forts on the San Juan River in Nicaragua in the far west of the Caribbean. The expedition had been badly planned and became a disaster, tropical diseases quickly leading to fatalities among the troops ashore. Nelson insisted on leading the boats taking the troops up the San Juan River but in a short time he too was struck down with fever and dysentery. The expedition had to be abandoned but when Nelson returned to his ship he found orders to return to Jamaica to take over command of the 44-gun ship JANUS. Tropical disease was by then rampant in the HINCHINBROKE and many died. When the ship got back to Jamaica in August 1780 it is said that all but fifty of her original complement of over two hundred had succumbed to the dreaded yellow fever.

The HINCHINBROKE foundered on the north coast of Jamaica, fortunately without loss of life, in January 1782.

His Britannic Majesty's 28-gun frigate "Hinchinbroke", formerly the French frigate "L'Astrée".
Commanded by Captain Horatio Nelson from June 1779 to May 1780.

Although violence was already smouldering across the colony as part of the struggle for independence, the local Nandi tribe had no interest or involvement in the Mau Mau. For five years the Gardners enjoyed a peaceful interlude two miles south of the Equator. Then they moved again, to the Rift Valley in central Kenya, and another idyllic five-year posting. With their two small children they lived at Nakuru, which some credit with the finest scenery and climate in the world. Their house stood on the side of an extinct volcano, with a crater fully two miles across. They looked out on to a huge soda lake with a shimmering pink fringe formed by tens of thousands of feeding flamingos. In his spare time the Regional Engineer was busy with his pictures of scintillating local landscapes and seascapes of the Indian Ocean. Mary says: "I was lucky. At weekends most of my friends were golf widows, but Derek was always painting beside me."

Then disaster struck. After an attack of tic typhus, Derek lost much of the hearing in his good ear. He was now very deaf and, he felt, unable to continue his career as a Chartered Civil Engineer. So in 1963, on the eve of Kenyan independence, the Gardners returned to England with their children and with no clear picture of what the future would hold. They were even unsure where they were going to live – or, as Derek puts it, his speech typically peppered with naval parlance, to "drop anchor permanently". Having previously enjoyed several months of home leave in a rented cottage near Southwold, they had a vague inkling for East Anglia. But while considering possible options, they took a lease on a house in Marlborough and then, with their son at school in Bath, found themselves gravitating towards Dorset. An ancient and fairly dilapidated thatched cottage was viewed in a village a few miles from Poole which they saw had the potential for a family base, with a programme of restoration and extension work to be overseen (and largely undertaken) by Derek. So far they have been

10. **His Britannic Majesty's 28-gun frigate "Albemarle"** *(detail opposite)*
Watercolour 10 x 14 ins, 24 x 36 cms Signed

Nelson served in "Albemarle", August 1781 to July 1783

The 28-gun frigate "ALBEMARLE"

Like the HINCHINBROKE this was another French prize. She was LA MENAGERE, captured as an armed store-ship in 1778. At that time the Royal Navy was outnumbered by ships of the French, Spanish and Dutch alliance all supporting the American colonies in their bid for independence. Any ship thought to be suitable for escort work was taken in hand and even a somewhat doubtful vessel like LA MENAGERE was commissioned for naval service.

Renamed ALBEMARLE the ship was commissioned in November 1779. For a year she served in the West Indies before coming home to undergo an extensive refit. In August 1781 she was recommissioned as a 28-gun frigate by Captain Horatio Nelson who remained in command of her for the next two years until, the American war being over, she was paid off in July 1783 and thereafter sold.

My painting shows the ALBEMARLE escorting a convoy in the North Sea on passage to Elsinore in November 1781 when Nelson was her captain.

His Britannic Majesty's 28-gun frigate "Albemarle",
under Captain Horatio Nelson, escorting the Baltic convoy 2nd November 1781.

at anchor there, very happily, for more than 40 years.

For a retired naval commander and colonial civil engineer having to come to terms with a serious disability, an approaching 50th birthday might have seemed more of a millstone than a milestone. But both Derek and Mary are made of sterling stuff, and possessed of a strong Christian faith. Armed with praise for the pictures he had exhibited in Kenya and London – and a prize he had won for an initial showing in America – an amateur painter determined to become a professional artist, working from an old garage in the garden. He would paint what he knew best and loved most: ships and the sea. But how to do it? Mary says: "It was very hard. Derek was a man who, with tremendous determination and staying power, refused to give in. We had to survive so he felt that he just had to progress with his painting. He began by trial and error – and I met several paintings coming out of the studio as I was coming in. One ended up on top of the rabbit hutch, and really it wasn't bad at all. But he said: 'If it's not good enough for me, then it's not good enough for anyone else.' To this day he is the toughest critic of his work."

With characteristic under-statement, Derek Gardner has written: "As an artist I am entirely self-taught. Looking back over some 50 years of painting I can see that sound technical advice early on would have saved me a lot of unnecessary experiment with colour mixing and so on, but even so I am convinced that no one can teach you to be an artist; that is something you have to develop yourself from such interests and enthusiasms as you have within you. Having said that, sound drawing with an understanding of the laws governing perspective is the foundation of good marine painting." In conversation in his studio, he airs his observation that those attending art schools so often tend to be unduly influenced by the people who teach them, even to the extent that students lose their originality. He

11. **His Britannic Majesty's 28-gun frigate "Boreas"** *(detail opposite)*
Watercolour 10 x 15 ins, 24 x 38 cms Signed

Nelson served in "Boreas", March 1784 to November 1787

The 28-gun frigate "BOREAS"

The BOREAS, one of six frigates of the MERMAID class, was built at Hull and launched in 1774. She was armed with 24 9-pounder guns and four 3-pounders. With war threatening in the American colonies she was sent on commissioning to the West Indies where she was to serve for the greater part of her twenty-eight years in the Royal Navy. Ten years later, in March 1784, after the vessel underwent an extensive refit at Woolwich, Nelson was appointed as her captain. He was then aged twenty-five. In May the ship sailed for Barbados where on arrival Nelson found he was the most senior captain and accordingly the second-in-command under the commander-in-chief Rear Admiral Sir Richard Hughes. They were an ill-suited pair, Nelson's strong sense of duty frequently clashing with the easy-going ways of his senior.

It was during his time as captain of the BOREAS that Nelson met and in March 1787 married Frances Nisbet, a young widow who was keeping house for her wealthy widowed uncle on the island of Nevis. Later that year the BOREAS was ordered to return to Portsmouth where in November the ship was paid off. For Nelson this was the beginning of eight years of half-pay unemployment which lasted until February 1793 when war again broke out with France and he was appointed to the AGAMEMNON.

His Britannic Majesty's 28-gun frigate "Boreas", launched July 1774,
was commanded by Captain Horatio Nelson from March 1784 to November 1787.

12. **Battle of the Glorious 1st June**
Watercolour 15½ x 27 ins, 38 x 69 cms Signed

The Battle of the Glorious 1st June, 1794

This was the first of the great naval battles of the French Revolutionary War. Due to a poor harvest and political disturbance France was becoming very short of food and in some places people were near to starvation. The government had purchased large quantities of grain in America which had been loaded into a hundred and seventeen merchant ships in the Chesapeake and by May 1794 the convoy was known to be at sea and on its way to France. The convoy was escorted by four ships-of-the-line and it was planned that the French fleet under the command of Admiral Villaret-Joyeuse would sail from Brest to cover it against attack by the British fleet.

The British Fleet under Admiral Lord Howe was at sea to the south-west of Brest when he heard that the French fleet had sailed and were no doubt heading west to protect the home-coming convoy. His flag was in the 100-gun QUEEN CHARLOTTE and with twenty-six ships-of-the-line and six frigates the Channel Fleet headed out into the Atlantic in pursuit of the enemy.

On 28th May when some five hundred miles to the west of Ushant, the French fleet was sighted some ten miles to windward. Howe sent five of his fastest ships under Rear-Admiral Pasley to reconnoitre which led to a partial action with the French rear in which the three-decker LA REVOLUTIONAIRE was severely damaged and lost 400 men. On 29th, the QUEEN CHARLOTTE with the LEVIATHAN and BELLEROPHON were in action with ships of the French rear and severely damaged three of them. The 30th and 31st were foggy. Howe was able to keep in contact with the enemy who skilfully edged away, protecting their damaged ships and at the same time allowing the slow-moving grain convoy to gain distance.

At dawn on 1st June the enemy fleet of twenty-five ships-of-the-line and fifteen frigates was sighted six miles distant to leeward heading west with a fresh southerly wind. Villaret-Joyeuse at the centre of the line with flag in the 120-gun MONTAGNE. The French ships opened fire at 9.30a.m. as the British fleet came down to attack. It was Howe's intention that each of his ships should break through the enemy line under the stern of her proper opponent and then engage from leeward. Anxious that the flagship should be the first to do so, he set the QUEEN CHARLOTTE's top gallants and let fall her foresail as an example to the fleet. Soon after ten o'clock he passed at close range under the stern of the MONTAGNE and fired a tremendous broadside along her gun-decks. Probably due to confusion over the meaning of the admiral's signal, only six of Howe's ships broke the French line – the majority continuing to engage their opponents from windward. The battle was a hard-fought affair, many ships in both fleets being heavily damaged and when it ended that afternoon eleven of the British ships were more or less dismasted as were twelve of the French. The outcome of this memorable action was the surrender of seven French ships-of-the-line, one of which, the gallant 74-gun VENGEUR, foundered within ten minutes of striking her flag.

The British fleet fought under the red ensign and the French under the flags of 1790, the only fleet action in which those flags were employed. In 1794 Lord Howe was an Admiral of the White but in order to avoid confusion in the smoke and heat of battle with the French flag, he ordered the British ships to wear the Red ensign. He was also at the time an acting Admiral of the Fleet and was therefore entitled to hoist a Union flag at his flagship's main.

says he always wanted his own voice, but quickly adds: "Although liking to be a little original, I make no claim for breaking new ground in what I do. I paint the sea, the sky and ships because I enjoy doing so and my wish is that my pictures will give to those who see them something of the enjoyment I have found in painting them."

*   *   *   *

Combining natural history and national heritage, England's tradition of marine painting may be said to date from the three Anglo-Dutch wars in the third quarter of the 17th century – contests over the latter's supremacy of the seas and its resulting riches from lucrative trading links. Wealth and patronage had allowed the arts to flourish. One big beneficiary was Willem van de Velde the Elder, a shipmaster's son born in Leiden around 1611, who went to sea as a boy and ever afterwards depicted the marine world in his pictures. The earliest

artist to accompany a fleet into action as an official recorder, he worked from a small craft to sketch nearby warships and fireships in dazzling detail. A namesake son in Amsterdam then used the battle drawings as notes for bravura pictures which were very popular with the men of prestige and power. In the winter of 1672-3, with the Dutch states in dire straits against the combined forces of France and Britain, the van de Veldes moved to London following the invitation of Charles II. Given generous allowances and a studio in Queen's House, overlooking Greenwich Park, they continued to view the scenes of naval battles, albeit from the opposing side. Their work, now on view in their old workshop as part of the National Maritime Museum collection, shows that they founded the marine painting tradition in their adopted country – a sequence of kindred talents spanning the centuries from Samuel Scott, Charles Brooking, Nicholas Pocock and Thomas Luny, to George Chambers, Thomas

13. **His Britannic Majesty's 64-gun ship "Agamemnon"** (detail opposite)
Watercolour 9 x 13 ins, 23 x 33 cms Signed

Nelson served in "Agamemnon", February 1793 to December 1796

The 64-gun ship "AGAMEMNON"

This famous ship was built on the Beaulieu River in Hampshire and launched in 1781. She was destined to have an active and distinguished career which to a large extent is reflected in the many Battle Honours accorded to her. These were: Ushant 1781; The Saintes 1782; Toulon 1793; Genoa 1795; Copenhagen 1801; Calder's action 1805; Trafalgar 1805 and San Domingo 1806.

When war with France again broke out in February 1793 Captain Nelson was called from retirement to commission her. He was then thirty-five years old. In May the vessel was ordered to proceed to the Mediterranean where Nelson remained in command for the next three years, greatly distinguishing himself and bringing fame to his ship. Promotion to commodore in 1796 saw the transfer of his broad pendant to the 74-gun ship CAPTAIN as the AGAMEMNON was by then badly in need of repair and had to return to England. As her Battle Honours indicate, the ship went on to see much service and action. She finally met her end in the far-off waters of the River Plate where, in 1809, she grounded on a shoal and despite every effort to keep her afloat she became a total loss.

His Britannic Majesty's 64-gun ship "Agamemnon", launched 1781,
commanded by Captain Horatio Nelson from February 1793 to May 1796.

Somerscales, William Lionel Wyllie and Montague Dawson. Derek Gardner, now the grand old man of British marine painting, is the latest in the line. Examples of his work are held by the national collection at Greenwich and the Royal Naval College at Dartmouth. His pictures are also prominent in private collections from America to South Africa and Australia, as well as in museums from Bermuda to Tenerife. He has had seven one-man exhibitions of his work in London since 1972 at the Polak Gallery, arranged by Robert and Stephen Jack, which unfortunately closed in 1999 after almost 150 years. He was elected a member of the Royal Society of Marine Artists in 1966 and had the great honour of being appointed a life-time Honorary Vice President of the society in 1988. In 1982 and 1984 he was a finalist in the Hunting Group Art Prizes competition organised by the Federation of British Artists. Gardner oils and watercolours have been reproduced in a series of books, from dictionaries of marine painters to titles such as Tall Ships by Gareth Rees (Phaidon, 1978), The Windjammers by Oliver E. Allen (Time Life Books, 1978), The Tall Ship in Art (Blandford, 1998) and Nelson's Ships by Peter Goodwin (Conway Maritime Press, 2002) from the latter of which much information has been obtained for the descriptive writings in this catalogue. The artist is also an Honorary Lay Patron of the Mission to Seafarers charity, donating an image for a Christmas card annually for more than two decades.

* * * *

Now beautifully restored and extended, the Gardner residence lies in a large garden of lawns and box hedges which has long been the couple's pride and joy. It offers a fine view down the valley, but not a glimpse of the sea. The harbour and marina at Poole are within easy reach, and a tour of the coast around Lyme Regis makes for a pleasant day trip, but there has never been any time for sailing

14. **His Britannic Majesty's 74-gun ship "Captain"** *(detail opposite)*
Watercolour 10 x 15 ins, 25 x 38 cms Signed

Nelson served in "Captain", June 1796 to May 1797

The 74-gun ship "CAPTAIN"

This is the ship in which Nelson carried out his courageous exploit at the Battle of St. Vincent on 14th February 1797 when he took the CAPTAIN out of the line to prevent the two divisions of the Spanish fleet uniting. His daring initiative succeeded and did much to bring about the victory which followed. The capture under the guns of the CAPTAIN of two powerful ships-of-the-line, the SAN NICOLAS of 80 guns and the SAN JOSEF of 112, when Nelson himself led the boarders, was a remarkable achievement. When it later became known in England, the feat brought fame to his name which has been a national glory ever since. For his outstanding service Nelson was made a Knight of the Bath.

The CAPTAIN was built on the Thames and launched in 1787. She saw much action during the French wars, being awarded Battle Honours for Toulon 1793, Genoa 1795, St. Vincent 1797 and Martinique 1809. She accidentally caught fire at Plymouth in 1813 and was destroyed.

His Britannic Majesty's 74-gun ship "Captain", launched 1787.

Derek G.M
GARDNER
1992

The Battle of St. Vincent, 14th February 1797

A French attempt to land 16,000 troops on the west coast of Ireland in January 1797 ended in disaster. The invasion fleet sailed from Brest in mid-winter and, as might have been expected, persistent gales led to complete failure and the loss of many men and ships.

Despite this misfortune the Ministry of Marine and the army continued to prepare plans for an invasion of England. The intention was that the ships at Brest would be reinforced by the fleets of Spain and Holland which, combined, would outnumber the Royal Navy's strength in the Channel.

In February 1797 Admiral Sir John Jervis with his flag in the VICTORY, was at sea near Cape St. Vincent with fifteen ships-of-the-line and five frigates watching for the appearance of the Spaniards who were believed to be coming out from Cadiz in an endeavour to join up with the French at Brest. On 14th February they were sighted, twenty-seven ships-of-the-line and twelve frigates sailing in two separate divisions a mile or two apart. By bringing his ships down between the approaching enemy divisions, Jervis saw the opportunity of engaging part of their fleet with the whole of his and although the Spanish lee division tried to break through and join up with the main division of their fleet to windward, they were repulsed and driven off. This is the situation at about midday which I have shown here.

Admiral Jervis gave the order for his fifteen ships to tack in succession. One by one they came round onto the same course as the main division of the Spanish fleet but by now somewhat astern of them. It was then that Commodore Nelson in the 74-gun CAPTAIN, sailing as the last but two in the line, realised that the enemy might still be able to join forces unless they were promptly brought to action and their course for doing so barred. He then independently and with much courage wore his ship out of the line and, supported by his friend Captain Collingwood in the 74-gun EXCELLENT, stood across the advancing Spanish ships and engaged them at close range. In carrying out this bold manoeuvre, the CAPTAIN reached the sixth ship of the enemy line which was none other than the flagship of the Spanish admiral, the SANTISSIMA TRINADAD of 130 guns. Needless to say the CAPTAIN was heavily damaged and as the British ships came up the action became general. Nelson drove his ship soon afterwards on to the stern of the 80-gun SAN NICOLAS and, boarding her at the head of his men, compelled her to surrender. Shortly afterwards the 112-gun SAN JOSEF ran aboard her and fire from her stern gallery killed several boarders. Nelson at once ordered his men to fire into her stern and with a shout of "Victory or Westminster Abbey" the commodore led his boarders into SAN JOSEF's main chains and in a few moments more was accepting the swords of the officers of this Spanish first-rate. The incident was later referred to as "Nelson's patent bridge for boarding First-Rates", the patent bridge being the SAN NICOLAS. In the course of the battle the 112-gun First-Rate SAVADOR DEL MUNDO and the 74-gun SAN YSIDRO were also captured, so bringing the action to a victorious end. It was a remarkable achievement by Admiral Jervis in gaining such success when outnumbered by almost two to one and great credit was accorded by him to Nelson whose perception and courage contributed so much to the victory. Sir John Jervis was made an Earl taking the title of St. Vincent and Nelson became a Knight of the Bath for his distinguished achievement.

The defeat of the Spanish fleet ended the threat of its combining with the French at Brest and the invasion fear was for the time being brought to an end.

15. **The Battle of St. Vincent, 1797**
    Watercolour 12½ x 24 ins, 30 x 61 cms Signed

The Battle of St. Vincent, 14th February 1797 – The Repulse of the Spanish Lee Division

(Left to right:) "Colossus" 74, "Irresistible" 74, Spanish Weather Division, "Orion" 74, "Prince George" 98, "Victory" 100, "Blenheim" 90, "Barfleur" 98, "Goliath" 74, "Egmont" 74, "Britannia" 100, "Namur" 90, "Principe de Asturias" 112, "Oriente" 74, "Firme" 74, "Glorioso" 74.

or idling in this particular household. For an artist who paused very briefly to celebrate his 90th birthday is happiest when at work. "People ask me whether I need to go to look at the sea before I paint my pictures," Derek says. "And the answer is: no, not any more." The sea has seeped into his soul.

He works in his now-spacious and airy studio all day and every day - standing at his easel beneath a huge north-facing window (with a view in exactly the opposite direction to the sea). After a break for lunch he puts in another afternoon painting session which may well end after 6pm, when Mary gently reminds him of the time. For he is all too likely to have lost track of the hours, such is his absorption in his pictures. Some say that those denied the use of one of the five senses may in time be compensated by the strengthening of another, and Derek Gardner's eye remains astonishingly sure. His hand is still steady. His enthusiasm and determination are entirely undimmed. He works below a favourite text from the popular song of a black American sage labouring on a Mississippi steam-boat:

You've got to get a Glory in the work you do,
An Hallelujah chorus in the heart of you,
Sing or paint a picture, dig or shovel coal,
You've got to have a Glory or the job lacks soul.

The ship-shape studio is also a nautical den – a captain's cabin. The walls are lined with naval books to which an exhaustive researcher makes constant reference. Also on display are the artist's seven war-time medals (including one award from Soviet Russia) and a portrait print of a certain heroic rear admiral signed Nelson & Bronte. Treasured maritime relics include a large square-headed nail recovered from the wreck of the Royal George, sunk at Spithead on August 29 1782, and the leg bone of a polar bear decorated with a Victorian scrimshaw carving of a whaling scene set against a fanciful backdrop of the erupting volcano of Krakatoa. On the easel an oil of the Battle of Trafalgar is slowly drying – a meticulous master informing me, without a hint of irony, that it shows the scene of the action "at about five past one".

16. **His Britannic Majesty's 38-gun frigate "La Minerve"** *(detail opposite)*
Watercolour 8 x 12 ins, 20 x 30 cms Signed

Nelson served in "La Minerve", December 1796 to February 1797

The 38-gun frigate "LA MINERVE"

The 40-gun French frigate LA MINERVE was captured in the western Mediterranean on 24th June 1795 by the frigates DIDO, 28-guns, and LOWESTOFFE, 32. She was repaired at Portsmouth and came into the Navy as a 38-gun Fifth Rate under her original name. She returned to the Mediterranean in 1796 and served there for the next six years until the Revolutionary War ended in 1802.

It was in December 1796 that Commodore Nelson was transferred temporarily from the CAPTAIN to LA MINERVE to supervise the evacuation of all British troops from the island of Elba. On his way, with the 32-gun BLANCHE, in company,

he encountered two Spanish frigates and after a fierce and damaging action forced the SANTA SABINA to surrender. His success was of short duration. The approach of a powerful Spanish squadron compelled Nelson to abandon his prize. Despite the heavy damage to his ship, he got clear in the darkness and, as he put it later, "escaped visiting a Spanish prison".

Soon after war with France resumed in 1803 LA MINERVE, when operating off Cherbourg, went aground in thick fog. Two French brigs approached and opened fire and although Captain Brenton managed to refloat his ship he was forced to surrender.

His Britannic Majesty's 38-gun frigate "La Minerve".

Derek G. M
GARDNER

17. **His Britannic Majesty's 74-gun ship "Theseus" leaving Portsmouth 9th September 1795** *(detail opposite)*
Watercolour 13 x 20 ins, 33 x 51 cms Signed

Nelson served in "Theseus", May to August 1797

The 74-gun ship "THESEUS"

The 74-gun ship-of-the-line THESEUS was built on the Thames at Blackwall, as one of the eight ships of the CULLODON class, and launched in 1786. She was laid up in ordinary for almost seven years before being put into commission in November 1793. The country was once again at war with France and the THESEUS, after serving for a few months with the Channel Fleet, was sent to the West Indies where she served until July 1795 when she came home to Portsmouth to be refitted. After this was completed she went again to the Channel Fleet until she sailed in March 1797 to join Admiral Sir John Jervis's fleet blockading Cadiz. Many of our ships had been damaged the previous month at the Battle of St. Vincent when Jervis had defeated the Spanish fleet, and no doubt the THESEUS was sent out to replace one of the ships forced back to England for repair.

Two months later, on 25th May, she became the flagship of Rear-Admiral Sir Horatio Nelson, Ralph Miller at the same time taking over as her captain. In July, on receiving a report that a Spanish treasure ship was lying at anchor in the bay off Santa Cruz, Tenerife, Jervis sent Nelson with eight ships to attack the town and take possession of the

ship. The expedition was a failure. Among many casualties, Nelson was severely wounded as he led the final attack on the town, his right arm having to be amputated on his return to the flagship. The ships withdrew and sailed back to report to the admiral off Cadiz who, on their arrival, at once sent the invalid Nelson home to England in a frigate.

In April 1798 Nelson, back on active service and with his flag in the 74-gun VANGUARD, rejoined Jervis who was now Admiral Lord St. Vincent. Anxious to obtain information about the large expedition assembling at Toulon for some unknown destination, St. Vincent sent Nelson with three ships to make a reconnaissance but serious storm damage to the VANGUARD delayed him, and meanwhile the expedition put to sea. Then followed weeks of frustration as Nelson, reinforced to thirteen ships-of-the-line, searched the eastern Mediterranean for his elusive enemy. The THESEUS was now one of the ships with Nelson's fleet which at last, on the afternoon of 1st August 1798, discovered Vice-Admiral Bruey's ships at anchor in Aboukir Bay. Nelson at once sailed in to attack and the ensuing Battle of the Nile

resulted in an overwhelming victory, with the virtual destruction of the French Mediterranean fleet and the isolation of their army in Egypt. The THESEUS was much damaged with many casualties, being hulled in more than seventy places. After repairs she returned to the eastern Mediterranean and between March and May 1799, with the 74-gun TIGRE Commodore Sir Sydney Smith won a further Battle Honour when she gave invaluable support to the defenders of the fortress at Acre on the Syrian coast when besieged by Bonaparte's invading army. The siege failed and the army was forced to return to Egypt after suffering heavy losses. Unfortunately during these operations an explosion of ammunition on the deck of the THESEUS killed forty of her men including Captain Miller. Great damage was done, the poop and the after part of the quarterdeck being blown to pieces.

She came home to refit in 1800 and in 1801 was once more sent to the West Indies where she remained until 1805. Her service from then on was chiefly keeping a watch on the French Atlantic ports. At the end of 1813 this fine ship was finally paid off and the following year she went to be broken up.

18. **His Britannic Majesty's 74-gun ship "Theseus"**
Watercolour 5½ x 8½ ins, 13 x 20 cms Signed

His Britannic Majesty's 74-gun ship "Theseus", launched 1786.

The Battle of Camperdown, 11th October 1797

Having been invaded by the French in 1795, the Netherlands were forced, as the Batavian Republic, to join France at war with Great Britain. For the next two years a strict watch was maintained by Admiral Adam Duncan's North Sea fleet on the Dutch navy anchored off the Texel. The fear was that the ships might succeed in getting to sea and sail to reinforce the French ships at Brest.

The mutiny at the Nore in the summer of 1797 had a grave effect on many of the ships under Duncan's command and for a time he found himself at sea off the Dutch coast with only two ships, making flag signals to an imaginary fleet over the horizon.

Early in October 1797, with discipline in his ships restored, he came to an anchor in Yarmouth Roads after being at sea for eighteen weeks. Scurvy had made its appearance and urgent repairs were needed after the long weeks at sea but within a few days of his arrival, on 9th October, the lugger SPECULATOR came in sight flying the urgent signal that the Dutch were out. Within three hours Duncan and his ships were at sea.

Vice Admiral de Winter had sailed from the Texel with twenty-five heavy ships and frigates heading south but, receiving news that the British were at sea in full strength, and as if realising that he might be caught by the once more efficient and well-practised ships of the North Sea fleet, he altered course back towards the Texel.

Duncan's frigates sighted the enemy on the morning of 11th October heading north some five miles off the Dutch coast opposite the village of Kamperduin. Admiral Duncan, with his flag in the 74-gun VENERABLE, at once decided to attack – doing so with his ships in two divisions, his own to windward and that of his second-in-command Vice-Admiral Richard Onslow in the 74-gun MONARCH, leeward. The battle which then took place was one of the hardest-fought during the long wars at sea with casualty lists in proportion to its severity. Unlike the French who usually aimed at masts and rigging the Dutchmen aimed their shot at the hulls to knock out guns and to kill men. Not a single lower mast of a British ship, not even a topmast was shot away. In both fleets many ships were struck by shot in all directions, the ARDENT for example was hit by no less than 98 round shot in her hull.

The battle began soon after noon. Four hours later with the surrender of de Winter's flagship, the 74-gun VRYHEID, the action came to an end Admiral Duncan finding himself in possession of no less than eleven out of eighteen heavy ships and frigates.

A few remarks about my painting may be of interest.

The British ships fought under both the blue and the red ensigns – those in Duncan's windward division wore the blue while those under Onslow wore the red. The Dutch ships hoisted the ensign of the Batavian Republic which was the well-known tricolour with the figure of Liberty in the hoist. The time is about 2p.m. At the right centre the VENERABLE is seen in close action with de Winter's flagship while in the centre of the painting I have shown the 64-gun ARDENT firing into the VRYHEID. On the left the POWERFUL, 74 guns, from Vice-Admiral Onslow's division is seen coming up to support Duncan. Soon afterwards she came round to starboard to engage the VRYHEID. On the extreme right, the 64-gun DIRECTOR is coming up, like the POWERFUL, after forcing the HAARLEM, 68 guns, to surrender.

19. **The Battle of Camperdown**
Oil on canvas 24 x 48 ins, 61 x 122 cms Signed

The Battle of Camperdown, 11th October 1797.

Peering hard and with apparent disapproval at the picture, having insisted that there is still a large amount of work to be done to avert a debacle, he says: "In naval battles of that period there was an enormous amount of smoke and to recognise friend from foe was very difficult, Many paintings don't show this. You have to organise your picture so that the smoke is blowing away from you rather than towards you. And this means that you often have to show the ships from the stern. In this particular scene, by way of contrast, the Temeraire is coming in from the bow on the extreme left of the picture."

It is such painstaking attention to detail – with a mastery of the complex rules of flags and pennants, for instance, as well as the precise choreography of each naval engagement – that has won Derek Gardner the praise of his professional peers, both sailors and painters alike. Alex A Hurst, the marine historian and author, has noted the embarrassment of being invited to find fault in a studio painting which seems to be flawless. "How inadequate can one feel! What can one possibly criticise?" he has written. "If I chance my arm and challenge a possible anachronism, he invariably has an immediate answer, since his research is so monumental and meticulous that one feels him to be living in the midst of a Napoleonic battle or painting with all the perspicacity of a wheeling albatross in the Southern Ocean as it eyes a running clipper which vanished long before he was born."

The final trick, of course, is then to impart all this information – while deliberately omitting much more – so that authenticity is confirmed without deadening the overall drama of the picture. Sails must be seen to ruffle and billow in the breeze, and ships to float in the water rather than being set fast in solid pigment. Clouds must appear to scud, and sun to glance on wood and canvas and to penetrate the grey-blue-green depths of the ocean. In short, the picture needs to give

20. **His Britannic Majesty's 74-gun ship "Vanguard"** *(detail opposite)*
Watercolour 10 x 14 ins, 25 x 36 cms Signed

Nelson served in "Vanguard", March 1798 to June 1799

The 74-gun ship "VANGUARD"

This fine ship-of-the-line was destined to become famous as Nelson's flagship at his great victory over the French Mediterranean Fleet at the Battle of the Nile in 1798.

She had been built on the Thames at Deptford and launched in 1787. When war broke out in February 1793 she sailed for the West Indies where she served until returning home for an extensive refit in 1797. When this was completed she was recommissioned under Captain Edward Berry and a few weeks later in March 1798 at Spithead she became the flagship of Rear-Admiral Sir Horatio Nelson. The VANGUARD sailed in April and after reporting to Admiral Lord St. Vincent off Cadiz, Nelson was sent with a small squadron to investigate reports of a large expedition preparing to sail from Toulon. Severe weather seriously damaged the VANGUARD which was forced to seek shelter off Sardinia to make repairs. The French ships put to sea and were not found until they were discovered at anchor in Aboukir Bay near the mouth of the Nile on 1st August 1798. Nelson immediately attacked and in the tremendous battle which followed he was wounded and his flagship severely damaged with heavy casualties. After temporary repairs the shattered ship and her damaged consorts eventually reached Naples in late September where further repairs were put in hand.

Nelson in the VANGUARD was much involved over the next nine months giving support to the Neopolitan kingdom against the French threat to Naples. His flag was finally struck in June 1799 when, as Rear-Admiral Lord Nelson, he transferred to the 80-gun FOUDROYANT.

The VANGUARD came home to Portsmouth at the end of the following year where she remained until May 1803 when the country again being at war with France, she sailed for the West Indies where she remained for the next two and a half years.

In 1807-08 she took part in the Baltic expedition which led to the bombardment of Copenhagen and the surrender of the ships of the Danish fleet. Returning to England the VANGUARD remained in commission until being finally paid off in 1811. After duty as a powder hulk Nelson's old flagship was broken up in 1821.

His Britannic Majesty's 74-gun ship-of-the-line "Vanguard"
seen here as the flagship of Rear-Admiral Sir Horatio Nelson, March 1798.

Derek G.M.
GARDNER

The Battle of the Nile, August 1798

Nelson, restored to reasonable health after losing his arm in the attack on Tenerife (see THESEUS p.70) and now a rear-admiral with his flag in the 74-gun VANGUARD, rejoined Jervis, now Lord St. Vincent, off Cadiz in April 1798. Within three days of his arrival, St. Vincent sent him with the 74-gun ALEXANDER and ORION and two frigates to the Mediterranean to obtain with great urgency information concerning a powerful force being assembled by the French at Toulon. Unfortunately a severe gale from the north-west struck his ships when some seventy-five miles off Toulon and the VANGUARD was dismasted. With the foremast gone and the main and mizzen topmasts overboard, the crippled ship was compelled to seek shelter to carry out repairs and was taken in tow by the ALEXANDER to anchor at St. Pietro, Sardinia. Nelson's ship was made seaworthy in a remarkable four days but his frigates, dispersed in the gale, had gone back to Gibraltar. A few days later he received news that the French expedition had left Toulon on 19th May, consisting of thirteen ships-of-the-line, several large frigates and almost two hundred transports packed with troops and supplies. The commander-in-chief of this formidable armament was General Bonaparte aboard the flagship of Vice-Admiral Brueys, the 120-gun L'ORIENT. The destination of this expedition was unknown but Nelson, although without frigates to reconnoitre, was convinced that Bonaparte had gone to Egypt. Off Sicily he learned that the French had taken Malta which strengthened his opinion that they were heading east.

He accordingly made all sail and arrived off Alexandria on 28th June but the enemy was not there, neither was there any account of them. He had arrived too soon. "Want of frigates," he cried would be found stamped on his heart. He sailed north to Syria hoping for information and thence back to Sicily and to Naples. From Sir William Hamilton, the British ambassador, he heard reports that confirmed his earlier judgement that Egypt must be the destination of the French expedition so once more his force of thirteen 74s and a 50-gun ship, the LEANDER, set sail for Alexandria. The ships arrived off the city at about ten in the morning and saw the harbour crowded with ships and the French flag flying on the city walls but there was no sign of the heavy ships of the navy which must have escorted the troopships. Such disappointment ended three hours later when the ZEALOUS signalled that seventeen ships-of-war, thirteen or fourteen of them lying in line of battle, were at anchor in Aboukir Bay some twelve miles or so to the east. The long search was over.

The British fleet at once headed east to Aboukir Bay which lies to the west of the Rosetta mouth of the Nile. Admiral Brueys had anchored his ships roughly in a north-west south-east line. The headmost ship at the western end, the GUERRIERE, was anchored close to a shoal, the other twelve ships astern of her lying in a slight curve along the line of shallowing water. There were nine ships of 74 guns, three of 80 guns and the flagship, the ORIENT of 120 guns. To oppose them Nelson had twelve ships of 74 guns and one of 50.

The British ships came in to attack in the late afternoon. Nelson's plan was to overwhelm the ships of the enemy's van and centre knowing there was little likelihood of help coming from their rear as the wind was blowing directly along their line. He also planned if possible to pass some of his ships round the head of the French line to attack them from their landward side which was unlikely to be manned and prepared for action. He gave Captain Hood of the ZEALOUS authority to attempt to do so and at about 6p.m. the ZEALOUS, supported by Thomas Foley's GOLIATH, successfully rounded Brueys's line. The ORION, under Captain Sir James Saumarez, and the THESEUS (Captain Miller) followed while the AUDACIOUS (Captain Gould) passed through between the GUERRIERE and the CONQUERANT, raking both ships as she did so. Nelson in the VANGUARD and the other ships following him came in and, anchoring by the stern on the seaward side of the enemy line, overwhelmed them with gunfire at point blank range on both sides. This is the situation at about 6.30p.m. which I have shown in my watercolour.

The battle went on all through the night. The huge flagship of Admiral Brueys caught fire and blew up in a shattering explosion at about 10p.m., needless to say with great loss of life. The British lost no ships but many were heavily damaged with severe casualties. Captain Westcott of the MAJESTIC was killed and Nelson was wounded along with three of his captains, Saumarez of the ORION, Darby of the BELLEROPHON and Ball of the ALEXANDER. Out of the thirteen French ships-of-the-line engaged in this great battle, nine were captured (of which three were later burnt), two were destroyed by fire or explosion and only two managed to get to sea and escape.

By this outstanding victory the French Mediterranean Fleet was virtually annihilated. Nelson's name became known throughout the whole of the Western world. He was raised to the peerage and had numerous honours bestowed on him while Bonaparte's dream that conquest of Egypt would be a stepping stone towards the seizure of British India lay shattered. His army was stranded in a distant land with little chance of receiving reinforcement or supplies.

The Battle of The Nile, 1st August 1798 – The Destruction of the French Van

(Left to right:) "Defence", "Minotaur", "Tonnant", "Orient", "Vanguard", "Franklin", "Souverain", "Aquilon", "Spartiate", "Orion", "Conquerant", "Goliath", "Audacious", "Guerriere", "Zealous".

the appearance of movement – and so to touch and transport the viewer. Here is Alex A Hurst again: "Marine painting is probably the most demanding of all forms of art. Some artists – the chosen few – are able to paint a sailing ship accurately and very beautifully, while some can portray a sea that is both liquid and really running true to life. Only in a tiny minority do the High Gods endow the gift of giving that ship her natural movement and her proper seat in the water which is so difficult to define, yet which makes or breaks a picture. Again the artist must satisfy the aesthete no less than the sailor (who will not tolerate inaccuracies) but, since the eye resembles a Box Brownie rather than a Leica, the self-discipline involved in omitting details which he knows to exist, although the eye would not see them, is enormous. At the same time he must not omit too much and the correct balance is very hard to achieve." Peter Stanford, President of the National Maritime Historical Society of the U.S.A, has

concluded: "The great thing is the way the ships sit in the water and the lovely effects of light at sea. All just great stuff!"

Derek Gardner works his magic by working very slowly. Each picture begins with a squared-up drawing, in which the key components of composition and perspective are carefully considered and then set out in a satisfying and historically accurate design. After that he applies wash after wash of transparent watercolour, or builds up glaze upon glaze of oil in the traditional manner to give a lively translucence and depth to his marine scenes. "I'm never in a hurry," he says. "Fools, after all, rush in. You can learn such a lot when you paint a new picture providing you take the time and the trouble – oils, in particular, are very hard to pull off. In mixed exhibitions you tend to see a fair few competent watercolours but often mediocre oils." One sweeping, swashbuckling Gardner oil painting of the 1797 Battle of Camperdown – one of the artist's undoubted

22. **His Britannic Majesty's 80-gun ship "Foudroyant"** *(detail opposite)*
Watercolour 9 x 15 ins, 23 x 38 cms Signed

Nelson served in "Foudroyant", June 1799 to July 1800, February to March 1801

The 80-gun ship "FOUDROYANT"

This powerful ship-of-the-line was built at Plymouth and launched in 1798. She was to have a life of almost a hundred years before being wrecked at Blackpool in June 1897 when employed as a boys' training ship.

When first commissioned in 1798 she sailed to Gibraltar where she joined the ships operating off Cadiz. Six months later she was sent to Palermo in Sicily where in June 1799 Rear-Admiral Lord Nelson hoisted his flag in her. In 1800 the FOUDROYANT played a leading part in two notable and successful encounters with French ships-of-the-line. The first, in February, resulted in the capture of the 74-gun GENEREUX when she was escorting a number of troop transports to Malta to relieve the garrison at Valetta. The second action six weeks later was an exceptionally hard-fought affair when the 80-gun ship-of-the-line GUILLAUME TELL was brought to action soon after breaking out from Malta in an attempt to reach Toulon. She was taken only after a noble defence against three ships – the FOUDROYANT, the LION, 64, and the frigate PENELOPE – an encounter which the naval historian William James summed up with the words: "A more heroic defence than that of the GUILLAUME TELL is not to be found among the records of naval action." The FOUDROYANT and the LION were both severely damaged and it was not until the end of April that Nelson was again able to hoist his flag in her. But two months later, on 28th June, his flag was finally struck when he left the ship at Leghorn to return to England.

The FOUDROYANT became Admiral Lord Keith's flagship a few weeks after Nelson's departure and so continued until July 1802 when with the ending of the Revolutionary War the ship returned home to Plymouth and was paid off. When hostilities resumed in 1803 the FOUDROYANT was recommissioned and went to the Channel Fleet and spent long and boring months at sea keeping watch over the French ports. In 1808 she was ordered to South America and served in those waters for the next four years, being based at Rio de Janeiro. She came home again to Plymouth, in 1812, where she was decommissioned and then laid up for several years before being taken in hand for a thorough refit. She then appears to have served as guardship at Plymouth for the next forty years. About 1860 she became a gunnery training ship until sold out of the navy in 1880.

His Britannic Majesty's 80-gun ship "Foudroyant",
flagship of Vice Admiral Lord Keith August 1800 to July 1802.

23. His Britannic Majesty's 80-gun ship "Foudroyant" *(detail)*
Watercolour 10½ x 14 ins, 25 x 36 cms Signed

His Britannic Majesty's 80-gun ship "Foudroyant",
flagship of Rear-Admiral Lord Nelson, June 1799 to July 1800.

masterpieces, illustrated in this volume and included in this exhibition – was almost four years in the making. He excels equally in oil and watercolour, and declines to express a preference for either form. "When I've been working in one medium for a certain period I just feel it is time to change tack," he says. "It's also very convenient to be able to work in watercolour while a big oil is drying!"

But in truth pictures start to float in this artist's head long before he first puts pencil to paper. After an exhaustive day standing in the studio, he likes to settle in an armchair beside a teetering pile of books – directing his reading to the artistic campaign ahead. He immerses himself in the immense, multi-volumed histories of the Royal Navy by William James and William Laird Clowes as well as in single titles such as Frank Howard's Sailing Ships of War, Frank Fox's Great Ships and David MacGregor's The Tea Clippers.

The result is that he is well versed in the smallest elements of the scene as well as the big picture. Discussing the differing tactics of national navies in the 17th, 18th and early 19th centuries, for instance, he notes: "When the Dutch went into battle they shot straight at ships as we did, trying to kill men. In contrast, when the French went in they tried to disable ships, by cutting away the rigging and the masts." This prompts me to suggest that France over this period may have possessed a greater humanity and a superior code of civilisation, to which the naval historian and artist smiles and replies: "In the Napoleonic Wars the French knew that their fleet was no match for the Royal Navy. So their objective was to disable British ships so that they were better able to escape. We had such an enormous fleet and our dockyard and repair facilities were unrivalled."

And having read up on his current subject, and drawn and painted the specific scene, the researcher turned artist then likes to conclude his project with a complementary essay. Although every picture really does tell

24. **His Britannic Majesty's 98-gun ship "St. George"** (detail opposite)
Watercolour 12 x 20 ins, 30 x 51 cms Signed

Nelson served in "St. George", March to July 1801

The 98-gun ship "St. GEORGE"

The 98-gun three-decker St. GEORGE, after seven years of war service, was withdrawn from the Channel Fleet to become the flagship of Vice-Admiral Nelson who had been appointed to be the thunderbolt second-in-command under the rather easy-going Admiral Sir Hyde Parker. A fleet was assembling off Yarmouth in February 1801 prior to sailing for Copenhagen to demand Denmark's withdrawal from a pro-French alliance with Russia and Sweden. Denmark's refusal led to the hard-fought Battle of Copenhagen. As the St. GEORGE was too deep to operate in the shoaling water off the city safely, she anchored with Parker's ships in deeper water to the north, Nelson hoisting his flag in the smaller 74-gun ELEPHANT. An armistice being agreed, the St. GEORGE thereafter remained for a time in the Baltic until returning to England with the fleet in June.

She appears to have been laid up in ordinary for a time before going over to Halifax and then came back two years later to serve once more with the Channel Fleet. In 1810 she returned to the Baltic as the flagship of Rear-Admiral Robert Reynolds. When standing by to escort a large convoy carrying naval stores of timber, pitch, tar and so on to England she dragged her anchors, drove ashore and lost her rudder. She managed to get clear after cutting away some of her masts and then jury-rigged set sail with the convoy. But on 11th December, when off the Jutland coast, the ship was wrecked in a hurricane with terrible loss of life. At the same time the 74-gun DEFENCE, which had been standing by to help, was also driven ashore and wrecked with tragic results. In the St. GEORGE 731 men were lost out of a complement of 738 and in the DEFENCE 583 out of 597, a total of 1314 men including Admiral Reynolds.

After the gale, ships in the North Sea bound for Copenhagen, March 1801

(Left to right:) "Edgar" 74, "Ardent" 64, "Monarch" 74, "St. George" 98 Flagship of Vice-Admiral Lord Nelson, "Alomene" 32.

a story, the words form a concise context – rather like an extra frame. And so the bulk of this book is properly devoted to the painterly and writerly portraits of Derek Gardner. But, by way of an introduction, here is the artist's description of a painting dating from the early 1970s – "Sir Lancelot" Passing the Eddystone: "The celebrated tea clipper Sir Lancelot was built in 1865 by Robert Steele at Greenock for James MacCunn who owned Guinevere and King Arthur. Like all the ships which came from Steele's yard, she was perfectly built and was constructed on the composite principle with teak planking over an iron framework.

"After a maiden voyage under an indifferent skipper, MacCunn was fortunate to obtain a splendid racing captain in Dick Robinson of the Fiery Cross and under her new master the little ship was able to show her paces. She was late in getting away from Woosung in 1867 but on the run home she overtook no fewer than 18 clippers which

had sailed before her and only the Taeping got in ahead of her. Her passage of 100 days was the best that year and Robinson's achievement made her name.

"In 1869, still under Robinson, she left Foochow on 17th July and although she was not the first clipper home that year (Titania had that honour) she reached London in 89 days which was the quickest passage ever made by a clipper between China and London.

"In 1876 she was cut down to a barque and her crew reduced. She loaded her last tea cargo in 1879 and after general trading to the East she was sold to Bombay owners in 1886. Nine years later, when under Persian ownership, she disappeared at sea and was presumed to have foundered in a cyclone in the Bay of Bengal."

Now it is time for me to depart after a day in the charming company of the Gardners. They share the contentment of a true partnership – Derek saluting the "wonderful

25. **His Britannic Majesty's 74-gun ship "Elephant"** (detail opposite)
Watercolour 6½ x 10½ ins, 15 x 25 cms Signed

Nelson served in "Elephant" during March and April 1801

The 74-gun ship "ELEPHANT"

The highlight of this 74-gun ship-of-the-line's career in the Royal Navy was undoubtedly her brief service as Vice-Admiral Nelson's flagship at the battle of Copenhagen in April 1801.

The ELEPHANT had been launched fifteen years earlier on the Hamble River in Hampshire, but four years went by before she was commissioned at Portsmouth. This period of activity was cut short to a mere six months on account of a severe epidemic affecting her crew and storm damage when lightning shattered her mainmast. She was then laid up in ordinary for the next nine years until again being put into commission in December 1799 under Captain Thomas Foley. This was almost seven years after the outbreak of the Revolutionary War and it remains a mystery why such a powerful ship was allowed to remain idle in wartime for such a lengthy period. After Foley commissioned her she was sent to the Channel Fleet for three months prior to being sent to join Admiral Sir Hyde Parker's Baltic expedition being assembled in the North Sea at Yarmouth. The ships sailed in March and anchored off Copenhagen on the 26th. The following day Nelson came on board from the 98-gun St. GEORGE, his choice of the smaller ship being due to her lesser draught in the shallow waters near the city. The battle was fought on 2nd April, a very fierce encounter with a brave and determined foe. The ELEPHANT suffered considerable damage to her hull and rigging as well as having twenty-two casualties. After the battle when repairs were completed many of the ships continued in the Baltic until July when, the political situation becoming more stable, they returned to England. In 1803 the ELEPHANT was sent to the West Indies where she served for the next four years, coming home in July 1807. She then had a lengthy refit and it appears she was not again commissioned until 1811. The Napoleonic War came to an end in 1815, the ELEPHANT remaining in service until 1818 when she was taken in hand and cut down to become a heavy frigate of 58 guns. She was broken up in 1830.

His Britannic Majesty's 74-gun ship "Elephant", launched 1786.

help that Mary is to me, not only on account of my deafness but for her constant encouragement over so many years and also for her gift as a constructive critic of my work".

Not for the first time I savour the good fortune of painters who, however historical their perspective and traditional their technique, are firmly moored in the present and the work in hand. And then there is all the looking forward to the next picture – and, in Derek's case, to the activities of a creative clan. For although he was the first artist in his family, his daughter is now a published writer and illustrator of gardening books and his landscape architect son is a gifted watercolourist. In addition, two grand-daughters are keen to progress in painting or photography, one starting out with an award in the national art competition for schools run to celebrate the Prince of Wales's 50th birthday. And so a painter in his tenth decade has one foot in a productive future. Although veteran artists carry all their experience within them, they remain enviably ageless. So that the sudden reminder of past times can come as a curious surprise. We have toasted current projects with beer before an excellent lunch, and only later do I notice that my tankard bears the slogan KYC Hill Adam Trophy 1956-7. (Derek served as Commodore of the Kisumu Yacht Club on Lake Victoria half a lifetime ago.)

My host is all set to drive me to the station, but the taxi is booked and when it finally appears the far-from-retiring naval commander helps in the steering of an about-turn and a tight manoeuvre. "Turn your stern round here!" he says to a bemused landlubber of a driver.

As I leave, amid much waving, I spy a rather ragged Union flag fluttering in the garden. It's a jaunty relic from the Queen's Golden Jubilee. Yes, the luck of artists who never take their flags down.

IAN COLLINS

26. **His Britannic Majesty's 32-gun frigate "Medusa"** *(detail opposite)*
Watercolour 4¼ x 7½ ins, 10 x 18 cms Signed

Nelson served in "Medusa", August 1801

The 32-gun frigate "MEDUSA"

In the summer of 1801 it was known that Napoleon was concentrating his army in Normandy in preparation for the invasion of England. Large numbers of shallow draught vessels were being built and held in readiness at Boulogne and other ports on the Channel coast. To counter the threat and largely to calm public anxiety, the Admiralty appointed Lord Nelson, the hero of the battles of the Nile and Copenhagen, to command all the naval forces from Suffolk round to Beachy Head. He hoisted his flag in the 32-gun frigate MEDUSA on 1st August 1801 and at once set in train his plan to attack the invasion vessels moored in the harbour at Boulogne. On the 4th, bomb-vessels opened fire but neither this attack nor a second ten days later achieved the success hoped for and in the face of a well-prepared enemy many casualties resulted. Nelson shifted his flag to the 38-gun frigate AMAZON later in the month, the MEDUSA continuing to serve in the Channel until the war came to an end six months later.

When war resumed in 1803 the MEDUSA was in the Mediterranean. Later, in October 1804 she was one of four frigates cruising in the approaches to Cadiz which were under orders to intercept four Spanish frigates known to be homeward bound from South America carrying treasure of great value. The four ships came in sight on 5th October. Although Spain at the time was neutral, its weak government was under considerable pressure from Napoleon to assist France financially. Knowing that the gold and silver and other valuables would be used to aid Britain's enemy, the Spanish admiral was called on to heave-to. Understandably he refused to do so and an action resulted which in a short time saw the more powerful British squadron victorious. One of the Spanish ships, the MERCEDES, blew up with great loss of life but the other three were taken together with their cargoes of enormous value. As a result of this high-handed action not surprisingly Spain soon afterwards declared war on England and in doing so became a somewhat reluctant ally of France. This had far-reaching consequences as only a year later the combined fleet of those two countries was overwhelmingly defeated by Nelson at the Battle of Trafalgar.

The MEDUSA went on to serve in the West Indies and in 1807 sailed with the expedition to South America in the unsuccessful combined operations with the army at Montevideo and Buenos Aires. She returned home in 1808 and from then on served chiefly in the Channel. She was finally paid off in 1813 then went to the breakers in 1816.

His Majesty's 32-gun frigate "Medusa", August 1801, with the flag of Vice-Admiral Lord Nelson at the fore.

The 100-gun ship "VICTORY"

Books have been written about this famous ship which was Vice-Admiral Lord Nelson's flagship when he died at the Battle of Trafalgar on 21st October 1805. She was designed by Thomas Slade and launched at Chatham in 1765. Today, two hundred and forty years later, she lies at Portsmouth in one of the oldest dry docks in the world and is still in commission as the flagship of the Second Sea Lord

The year of 1765, when she was launched, was a time of peace in that war-beset century and since there was no requirement in the navy for heavy ships, she was laid up and not put in commission until 1778 when we were again at war with France. She became the flagship of Admiral Augustus Keppel in command of the Channel Fleet. On 27th July 1778 her guns opened fire for the first time in anger at the Battle of Ushant, a hard fought but indecisive encounter with a powerful French fleet in which the VICTORY was considerably damaged. In December 1781 she was Rear-Admiral Richard Kempenfelt's flagship at what became known as the Second Battle of Ushant when a large French convoy taking troops and supplies to the West Indies was intercepted and some thirty ships and 1500 men were captured.

In the course of the French wars of the late eighteenth and early nineteenth centuries, the VICTORY was awarded the following Battle Honours: Ushant, July 1778, flagship of Admiral Augustus Keppel; Ushant, December 1781, flagship of Rear-Admiral Richard Kempenfelt; Toulon, August 1793, flagship of Vice-Admiral Lord Hood; St. Vincent, February 1797, flagship of Admiral Sir John Jervis; Trafalgar, October 1805, flagship of Vice-Admiral Lord Nelson; Baltic, 1808, flagship of Vice-Admiral Sir James Saumarez.

During the ten years of peace which followed the end of the American War of Independence in 1783, the VICTORY spent much of the time laid up in ordinary. When war broke out in February 1793 she was commissioned and sent to the Mediterranean to be the flagship of Vice-Admiral Lord Hood blockading Toulon. The town had strong royalist sympathies and after negotiations it was arranged that the naval base be handed over to the British admiral. The arrival of a republican military force brought the occupation of the harbour to an end. As the British withdrew, fourteen ships were destroyed including one of 80 guns, and sixteen brought away which included one of 120 guns.

In 1796 Spain declared war. The combined naval forces of France and Spain then posed a serious invasion threat especially against Ireland where they could expect some help from a disaffected population. Admiral Sir John Jervis, with his flag in the VICTORY, encountered a strong Spanish fleet at sea on 14th April 1797 and soundly defeated it at the Battle of St. Vincent, Nelson's courageous initiative largely

27. **His Britannic Majesty's 100-gun ship "Victory"** *(detail opposite)*
Watercolour 10 x 15 ins, 25 x 38 cms Signed

Nelson served in "Victory", May 1803 to October 1805

contributing to the success of that day. At the end of the year the VICTORY came home to undergo an extensive refit at Chatham. It was not until April 1803 that she was again commissioned and in May sailed for the Mediterranean where she hoisted Vice-Admiral Lord Nelson's flag as Commander-in-Chief. The main duty of his ships was the blockade of Toulon where the French fleet under the command of Admiral Villeneuve, lay at anchor. In April 1805 they escaped and unknown to Nelson sailed for the West Indies. A report of this finally reached Nelson who at once set sail to the Caribbean. Villeneuve, hearing that Nelson was in pursuit, headed back to Europe where his ships anchored at Cadiz following an action with a British force under Admiral Calder. The VICTORY returned home to Portsmouth for a much-needed refit before sailing on 15th September to Cadiz where Nelson resumed command of the fleet, blockading Villeneuve's Franco-Spanish ships lying there at anchor. In October Napoleon's impatience forced him to put to sea which, on the 21st, resulted in the great battle off Cape Trafalgar where seventeen of

his ships were captured.

The VICTORY was heavily damaged and after repairs at Gibraltar to make her seaworthy she eventually came home to Spithead and anchored on 5th December. Later that month she was taken to Chatham to undergo further repairs to her ageing hull and to have her armament somewhat reduced by fitting lighter-weight guns.

After her long refit the VICTORY was recommissioned in 1808. As the flagship of Vice-Admiral Sir James Saumarez she was sent to Spain to take part in the evacuation from Corunna of General Sir John Moore's hard-pressed and retreating army. She returned to England early in 1809. In May she sailed for the Baltic with a powerful squadron of eleven ships-of-the- line and five frigates to support Sweden in the war against Russia. When the severe cold of the Baltic winter set in, most of the ships, including the VICTORY, returned home to refit. Rear-Admiral Yorke temporarily replaced Saumarez and sailed with troops to Lisbon to reinforce the army fighting under the command of general Sir Arthur Wellesley, later Viscount Wellington. On returning she

again hoisted the flag of Vice-Admiral Saumarez and in April 1811 sailed to resume operations in the Baltic where she continued to serve until the autumn of 1812 when the ships were ordered home.

The VICTORY headed for Spithead where on 1st December she dropped her anchor. This was the end of her sea-going career and shortly afterwards she entered Portsmouth harbour to decommission. She was laid up until 1823 when she was commissioned to serve as harbour guardship for a time and flagship of the Port Admiral. She lay at anchor as the flagship of numerous admirals over the years off Gosport. The centenary of the Battle of Trafalgar in 1905 brought the old ship to the public's notice and proposals were discussed for restoring her to her Trafalgar appearance but it was not until after the First World War that she was taken in hand as a result of a successful national appeal launched by the Society for Nautical Research. She entered the dry dock in January 1922 and there she has figured as a national monument for the past eighty-three years, miraculously surviving the air raids on Portsmouth during the last war.

His Britannic Majesty's 100-gun ship "Victory", flagship of Vice-Admiral Lord Nelson,
at anchor off the Isle of Wight on 14th September 1805.

28. **His Britannic Majesty's 100-gun ship "Victory"** *(detail)*
Watercolour 13 x 19 ins, 33 x 48 cms Signed

His Britannic Majesty's 100-gun ship "Victory", flagship of Vice-Admiral Lord Nelson.

The Battle of Trafalgar, 21st October 1805

The Battle of Trafalgar is one of the great milestones in our long national history. In four and a half hours the British fleet under Vice-Admiral Lord Nelson, with his flag in the 100-gun VICTORY, utterly defeated the more numerous Combined Fleet of France of Spain under the command of the French Admiral Pierre Villeneuve.

On sighting the enemy at dawn some nine miles to the east, Nelson formed the British fleet into two roughly parallel lines, the northerly weather line led by the VICTORY and the lee line about a mile away to the south led by Vice-Admiral Collingwood's flagship the ROYAL SOVEREIGN. There was a light wind from the westward which took the British ships slowly down at a walking pace to engage the Combined Fleet heading in a somewhat ragged formation towards the north. The battle began at about midday when the ships of the Combined Fleet opened fire on the ROYAL SOVEREIGN as she approached to break through the line under the stern of the 112-gun SANTA ANNA. Nelson in the VICTORY headed to pass under the stern of Villeneuve's flagship, the BUCENTAURE. Broadsides from the allied line brought down her mizzen topmast, tore her sails to shreds and shattered her wheel as she continued to forge ahead. Then just after one o'clock, she passed under the French flagship's stern, her larboard guns double and even treble-shotted firing into the great cabin windows, wrecking guns and killing scores of men.

The painting shows the VICTORY just after she had fired that first broadside. Her starboard guns are firing into

29. **The Battle of Trafalgar, 1805** *(and front cover)*
Oil on canvas 24 x 40 ins, 61 x 102 cms Signed

(Left to right:) "Temeraire" 98, "Santissima Trinidad" 136, "Bucentaure" 80, "Cornelie" 40, "Victory" 100, "Neptune" 80, "Redoubtable" 74, "San Justo" 74.

the French 74-gun REDOUBTABLE which soon afterwards came close alongside and from whose fighting top the fatal shot was fired which struck Nelson as he paced the VICTORY's deck with Captain Hardy. On the extreme left the larboard guns of the 98-gun TEMERAIRE, the VICTORY's next astern, are firing into the Spanish SANTISSIMA TRINIDAD sailing next ahead of the BUCENTAURE and, with 136 guns, the largest ship afloat at that time. Ahead of the VICTORY is the French NEPTUNE, 80, whose larboard guns did much damage to the VICTORY as she raked her. On the far right is the Spanish 74-gun ship SAN JUSTO.

30. **The Battle of Trafalgar, 1805**
Watercolour 14½ x 26 ins, 36 x 66 cms Signed

Horatio Nelson

1758	29 September	Born at Burnham Thorpe, Norfolk.
1770	27 November	Enters as midshipman in the *Raisonnable*.
1773	June to September	Serves on expedition to the Arctic.
	November	In the East Indies.
1775		American War of Independence begins.
1778		Appointed Lieutenant.
1779		Appointed Post-Captain.
1780		Takes part in ill-fated attack in Nicaragua.
1782	April	Sails to Quebec.
	November	On convoy duty off New York.
1783	3 September	American War of Independence ends.
1785	2 May	Meets Frances Nisbet in the West Indies.
1787	11 March	Marries Frances Nisbet.
1788		On half-pay unemployment in Norfolk.
1793	6 January	Re-employed by the Admiralty.
	September	First visits Naples and meets the Hamiltons.
1794	12 July	Loses right eye at Calvi, Corsica.
1796	1 March	Promoted to Commodore.
1797	14 February	Plays distinguished role at Battle of Cape St. Vincent.
	20 February	Promoted to Rear-Admiral.
	17 May	Created Knight of the Bath.
	24 July	Loses right arm at Santa Cruz, Tenerife.
1798	1 August	Destroys French fleet at Battle of the Nile.
	22 September	Arrives in Naples.
	6 November	Created Baron Nelson of the Nile.
1799	August	Created Duke of Brontë by King Ferdinand IV of Naples.
1800	6 November	Returns to England with the Hamiltons.
	8 November	Reunited with Lady Nelson.
1801	1 January	Promoted to Vice-Admiral.
	5 February	Daughter, Horatia, born to Emma Hamilton.
	2 April	Leads attack at Battle of Copenhagen.
	22 May	Created Viscount Nelson of the Nile and Burnham Thorpe.
	18 September	Buys Merton Place, Surrey.
1803	6 April	Sir William Hamilton dies.
	16 May	Appointed Commander-in-Chief, Mediterranean Fleet.
1804	14 December	Blockades Toulon.
		Spain declares war on Britain.
1805	January-February	Pursues French fleet.
	18 August	Returns to England and to Merton.
	14 September	Rejoins the *Victory*.
	21 October	Killed at the Battle of Trafalgar.
1806	9 January	State funeral at St. Paul's Cathedral.

Epilogue

by Ian Collins

Nelson's state funeral saluted the man who had secured British naval supremacy – also distracting mourners from the dreadful news of Napoleon's victory at Austerlitz. A decade later the menace was finally vanquished on land at Waterloo, after which Bonaparte was transported by ship to St Helena.

Trade had increased dramatically in Nelson's lifetime – by 1794 Britain was buying nine million pounds of tea alone – and the rise of a mighty mercantile fleet increased the need for a Royal Navy to protect it. Surging imports and exports fuelled our industrial revolution. Territory was being bought up to protect far-flung trading posts, the East India Company already with its own army and navy, so that our small islands in north-west Europe gained economic muscle and, ultimately, via contract and conquest, the greatest empire the world has ever seen.

Steam-powered vessels, more independent of tide, winds and currents, floated from the early 1800s, and Britain also helped to pioneer awesome advances in naval armaments – iron and steel-armoured ships, torpedoes, submarines. After a Victorian policy to maintain a navy as large as those of the two nearest challengers combined, a fierce naval race with Germany was won by 1914. So an endless supply of men flowed freely to France and Flanders in World War One. The upstart German fleet was scuttled at Scapa Flow in 1919.

Although the inter-war period saw the Royal Navy buffeted by slump at home, rivalry abroad and the first winds of change to tear into the imperial fabric, Britain still had the world's largest fleet in 1939. Our security on the seas allowed twin marvels, the first defensive and the second invasive: Dunkirk and D-Day.

In 1945 the Royal Navy had almost 900 major warships and 866,000 personnel, with the Merchant Navy (which had suffered more World War Two casualties than any of the the Armed Services) also vast and vital. Although the fighting force was to be steadily diminished, and the field of operation reduced, firepower reached record levels with nuclear weapons in submarines.

Savage naval cuts mooted in 1982 were abandoned after an Argentine invasion of the Falklands and the raising of a Task Force to rescue islands 8000 miles from Britain. The Royal Navy played a key role in the 1991 Gulf War, and has patrolled close to many trouble spots since then – as near as 12 miles to land is still international waters so there is no need for diplomatic clearance to be there.

The sea is our national border, on which more than 90% of our imports and exports still travel. As over three-quarters of the world's countries have coastlines, shipping will remain the crucial form of trading transport.

Today the Royal Navy is a versatile fighting force spanning land, air and sea with its own ships, submarines, aircraft and soldiers (Royal Marines). Its roles include conflict and peace-keeping, humanitarian aid, anti-drug patrols, search and rescue, policing UK fishing grounds and oilfields, oceanographic surveys, protecting the marine environment and providing the nation's nuclear deterrent. Nelson would be amazed.

His Britannic Majesty's 38-gun frigate "SHANNON"

The SHANNON was one of the most famous and successful frigates of the Napoleonic War period.

On 1st June 1813 she defeated and captured the United States frigate CHESAPEAKE, a ship of almost identical size and armament, in an action fought off Boston. Although it lasted only fifteen minutes it was one of fiercest frigate actions recorded, resulting in heavy casualties in both ships. Captain Philip Broke of the SHANNON was severely wounded when he led his boarders on to the CHESAPEAKE's deck. Captain James Lawrence of the CHESAPEAKE died of his wounds four days later when on board the SHANNON on her way back to Halifax.

The watercolour drawing of the SHANNON shows her with the 38-gun frigate TENEDOS in company in April 1813 soon after they had left Halifax on their way south to take up their station watching Boston. The TENEDOS was later detached to operate off Cape Sable and was not in the area when the battle took place on 1st June.

The SHANNON was one of the numerous LEDAS class and was launched in May 1806.

31. **His Britannic Majesty's 38-gun frigate "Shannon"**
Watercolour 4¼ x 7½ ins, 10 x 18 cms Signed

His Britannic Majesty's frigate "Shannon", 38 guns, launched May 1806.

The California Clipper "SOUTHERN CROSS"

British wind-driven ships of the 1860s and 1870s were increasingly being built of iron, but in America builders along the New England coast still held to the old traditions of constructing vessels from wood.

The ship SOUTHERN CROSS, shown in this painting rigged with double topsails and a skysail at her main, is a fine example of a timber-hulled full-rigged ship sent afloat from a now long-forgotten shipyard at Boston. She was launched in 1868 for the rapidly-expanding California grain trade based at San Francisco which called for strongly-built vessels to fight their way round Cape Horn, with good cargo capacity and a fair turn of speed.

By 1868 San Francisco was a world-renowned port where up to 250 ships came in each year to load grain and barley. It had become a busy deep-water port following the discovery of gold in California twenty years earlier when tens of thousands of people, on hearing the news, headed for San Francisco and, once ashore, made for the mines and the prospect of a quick fortune. Before the Gold Rush, San Francisco had been nothing but a sleepy trading post

visited by a handful of ships a year. The population of California was small and scattered and was quite unable to provide for the needs of the thousands of newcomers who were continually arriving. The new arrivals produced gold but little else, so much food and the numerous requirements of daily life had to be brought over thousands of miles of salt water from the manufacturing centres around New York and Boston. Although things had improved by 1868, clippers like the SOUTHERN CROSS were now sailing to San Francisco each year to load grain and barley, carrying on the outward passage all manner of articles which California needed for its growing population.

These fine ships, built in Maine, Massachusetts, New Hampshire and Connecticut, came to be known as Down Easters. Their building began after the end of the Civil War in 1865. In the twenty-five or thirty years of their trading life, before it came to an end with the competition of steam, they were known in ports all over the world. But it is chiefly as a Cape Horner that the Down Easter is remembered.

32. American Clipper "Southern Cross"
Oil on canvas 17½ x 23½ ins, 43 x 58 cms Signed

Heigh-Ho and up she rises, the Tea Clipper "WYLO"

The British tea clippers were queens of the tea trade with China for something like thirty-five years before the opening of the Suez Canal in 1869 brought their reign to an end.

Speed was everything with the tea clippers and it was every captain's ambition to be chosen as one of the ships to load the new season's teas at Foochow or one of the other ports. Then the aim was to outsail all rivals and secure the honour and the prize paid to the first ship to dock each year at London at the end of the 17,000 mile passage from China.

The CUTTY SARK, in her dry dock at Greenwich, is the sole survivor of those beautiful, yacht-like merchantmen but the names and achievements of many of them are still remembered 140 years on.

In this painting I have shown the tea clipper WYLO homeward bound in 1870. She was then a new ship having been built at Greenock by the celebrated firm of Robert Steele & Co., from whose slipways had been launched such famous clippers as the ARIEL, SIR LANCELOT, TITANIA and LAHLOO.

The WYLO traded for many years with China and in the East. In his book The Great Days of Sail, Captain Andrew Shewan describes the WYLO as speedy but designed to carry a fair cargo of tea so she was not quite so fast as some of the other thoroughbreds which Steele had sent afloat.

Later, after fifteen years, the London shipowners Killick Martin & Co, sold her and she passed to Canadian interests and it was under Canadian ownership when she was finally lost in collision in 1888.

33. Tea Clipper
Oil on panel 14¼ x 23¾ ins, 36 x 58 cms Signed

Ships of the Fifth Battle Squadron, 1916

The five ships of the QUEEN ELIZABETH class, launched between 1913 and 1915, served in both the world wars and will probably be remembered as the most famous class of all British battleships.

The four shown here at anchor in the Firth of Forth in May 1916 are the VALIANT, WARSPITE, MALAYA and BARHAM, the QUEEN ELIZABETH at the time being in dockyard hands for refitting at Rosyth. They formed the Fifth Battle Squadron which fought in support of Vice-Admiral Beatty's battle-cruisers at the Battle of Jutland on 31st May 1916, the BARHAM on the right being the flagship of Rear-Admiral Evan Thomas.

All five ships came through the First World War. During the inter-war years the QUEEN ELIZABETH, WARSPITE and VALIANT were taken in hand to undergo alterations which amounted to almost a complete rebuilding while the BARHAM and MALAYA had limited modernisation to maintain their front-line standard.

All five ships gave fine and often outstanding service in the Second World War but the BARHAM was lost in 1941 when she was torpedoed by a U-boat in the Mediterranean and blew up with, sadly, a great loss of life.

The ships' main armament was eight 15-inch guns in four twin turrets with a secondary armament of 6-inch guns. Under normal full power they had a maximum speed of 23 knots and, when new, a displacement tonnage of 27,500.

34. Ships of the Fifth Battle Squadron
Oil 10 x 20 ins, 25 x 50 cms Signed

The "SUPERB" at Scapa, 1916

This watercolour drawing of the battleship SUPERB, seen from a point fine on her port bow, shows her under way at Scapa Flow in 1916 with one of the INVINCIBLE class battle-cruisers in the mist astern.

The SUPERB was built on the Tyne and completed in 1909, five years before the outbreak of the First World War. She was one of three ships of the BELLEROPHON class, the third being the TEMERAIRE, so all three carried the names of ships which served under Nelson at the Battle of Trafalgar. The SUPERB served throughout the war with the Grand Fleet and fought at the Battle of Jutland in the 4th Battle Squadron.

The BELLEROPHON class was almost a repeat of the famous DREADNOUGHT, which as a new battleship broke with the past by having superior armament, speed and protection to any battleship in the world. The ships were armed with ten 12-inch guns in five twin turrets, driven by steam turbines with a maximum speed of twenty-two knots.

35. **"Superb" at Scapa Flow, 1916**
    Watercolour 6¾ x 8½ ins, 15 x 20 cms Signed

Heavy ships in the Fleet anchorage at Scapa Flow, March 1940

Scapa Flow in the Orkneys was the main base of the Battle Fleet in both world wars. It is an almost land-locked area of about forty-five square miles, sheltered from both Atlantic and North Sea gales.

In the early days of the Second World War its security was compromised by the sinking of the battleship ROYAL OAK, when at anchor, by a U-boat which daringly entered the Flow through a channel which was thought to be blocked. This rendered Scapa quite unfit as a base for the fleet until the entrances were made secure and adequate anti-

aircraft batteries erected on the islands. These measures were not completed until March 1940 when the heavy ships were able to return from their temporary base on the west coast of Scotland at Loch Ewe.

This painting shows from left to right five ships of the Home Fleet: the RENOWN, RODNEY (flagship of the Commander in Chief), REPULSE, HOOD and VALIANT in the anchorage in March 1940 when the defences had been completed.

36. **World War Two, heavy ships, Scapa Flow**
Oil 9½ x 23 ins, 23 x 58 cms Signed